Just for a Thrill

OTHER MUSIC BOOKS BY JAMES L. DICKERSON

Colonel Tom Parker: The Curious Life of Elvis Presley's
    Eccentric Manager
Faith Hill: Piece of My Heart
Dixie Chicks: Down-Home and Backstage
Women On Top: The Quiet Revolution That's Rocking the
    American Music Industry
That's Alright, Elvis: The Untold Story of Elvis's First Guitarist
    and Manager, Scotty Moore (*written with Scotty Moore*)
Goin' Back to Memphis: A Century of Blues, Rock 'n' Roll and
    Glorious Soul

Just for a Thrill

Lil Hardin Armstrong
First Lady of Jazz

JAMES L. DICKERSON

Cooper Square Press

Published by Cooper Square Press
An Imprint of the Rowman & Littlefield Publishing Group
150 Fifth Avenue, Suite 817
New York, New York 10011

Distributed by National Book Network

Library of Congress Cataloging-in-Publication Data

Dickerson, James.
    Just for a thrill : Lil Hardin Armstrong, first lady of jazz /
James L. Dickerson.
        p. cm.
    Includes bibliographical references and index.
    ISBN 0-8154-1195-2 (cloth : alk. paper)
    1. Armstrong, Lil Hardin, 1902–1971.   2. Women jazz musicians—
United States—Biography.   I. Title.

ML420.A755   D53   2002
781.65'092—dc21
[B]   2001056165

♾™   The paper used in this publication meets the minimum requirements of
American National Standard for Information Sciences—Permanence of Paper
for Printed Library Materials, ANSI/NISO Z39.48–1992.
Manufactured in the United States of America.

To my niece, Janet McCaskill

Contents

Acknowledgments

I would like to thank the following people for their help with this book: the staff at the Public Library of Nashville and Davidson County; the staff at the Jean and Alexander Heard Library at Vanderbilt University; my editor at Cooper Square Press, Michael Dorr; also at Cooper Square, Michael Messina and Ross Plotkin; Michael Cogswell and Peggy Schein at the Louis Armstrong House and Archives; Wayne Johnson at the Chicago Crime Commission; Tammy Helm at Universal Music Publishing Group; the Federal Bureau of Investigation for releasing its files on Louis Armstrong and Joseph Glaser; Ed Frank of the Mississippi Valley Collection at the University of Memphis; Harriet Choice for her recollections of a sad day; and Mark Cave at the Williams Research Center in New Orleans.

Introduction

The first sheet music I ever purchased was "Struttin' With Some Barbecue."

Growing up in the Mississippi Delta in the late 1950s and early 1960s, I was surrounded by music. Bluesman Sam Chatmon often performed on the street corners of my hometown during the week. Jimmy Reed, Little Milton, Bobby "Blue" Bland, and others headlined on the weekends at the clubs across the tracks.

I was much too young—and much too white—in that era of racial segregation to be admitted to the gritty nightclubs where they performed, but their music traveled easily in the night air and could be enjoyed from the branches of a tree at a discreet distance.

As much as I liked the blues and rock 'n' roll, it was jazz that inspired me to want to make music of my own. I purchased albums by Dave Brubeck, Duke Ellington, Louis Armstrong, and Mose Allison at an age when my classmates were hooked on Elvis Presley and Rick Nelson.

One day, while talking to my high-school music teacher, James Harvey, about jazz, I learned his deepest, darkest secret: during the 1930s, he had played trumpet in jazz bands across the South (I later found out he was a minor legend). He eventually gave all that up for the security of a job as a high school music and science teacher.

The more we talked, the more interested he became in his own history as a jazz musician. After weeks of persuasion, he finally agreed to meet on weekends with me and a couple of other students at his home to play jazz. I will never forget the day I first heard him play. There was something magical about the way he brought the trumpet to his lips and slipped into those first notes. There was a look in his eyes that I will never forget.

When he played, it was the most incredible sound I had ever heard . . . so smooth and soulful. It was hard to believe that the white-haired man making that incredible music was my high school teacher.

One day, tired of the arrangements we were playing, I ordered some sheet music from a mail order catalog. The best of the lot was titled "Struttin' With Some Barbecue." I never paid any attention to who wrote the song. I was too busy sweating out the trombone part to care about authorship.

Some thirty years later, while I was researching my first book, *Goin' Back to Memphis*, I discovered that the author of "Struttin' With Some Barbecue" was Lil Hardin Armstrong, a native of Memphis. She was tucked away in the footnotes of jazz history, an afterthought to the life of her husband, Louis Armstrong.

Since my history of Memphis music required a section on Lil Hardin Armstrong, I dug deeply to find out what I could about her. The more I learned, the more I wanted to know. That was not easy because jazz writers, from the beginning, have not been kind—or even remotely fair—to female jazz musicians. Often, the information I discovered was incorrect. On a couple of occasions, I passed that misinformation along to my readers—and for that I apologize.

Lil had a habit of misrepresenting her age, always on the side of youth. Jazz writers, because they were typically hostile to female musicians, made no effort to document their lives at anywhere near the levels they did for male musicians, and they seldom made an effort to verify information about female musicians. That pleased Lil, insofar as her age was concerned, but it ultimately damaged her career as a serious artist because it led to other, less flattering distortions of fact concerning her music

All music is a reaction to environment and cultural history: you cannot write effectively about that music without living it. So much jazz history has been written by individuals who know little about the culture of the South and the interpretations they present are often flawed, I think, because of that lack of understanding.

Throughout jazz history there has been a sexist bias against women. Most of the people who have written jazz history have been white males, and certainly I belong in that group. While I don't apologize for being a white male, I do apologize for the chauvinistic drivel that other white male writers have injected into the study of jazz. The tendency for the past half-century has been to ignore the contributions of women like Lil Hardin Armstrong, and that is deplorable.

Typical of the hostility toward women in jazz are these comments from a Jazz Age era writer for *Down Beat* magazine: "Why is it that outside of a few sepia females the woman musician never was born capable of sending anyone further than the nearest exit? . . . You can forgive them for lacking guts in their playing but even women should be able to play with feeling and expression and they never do it."

When you think about it, jazz is essentially a feminine form of expression. Just as women use more words than men do when expressing themselves in conversation and engage in a less linear thought process, so do jazz musicians—and they do so with a typically feminine goal of introspective expression. The top male jazz players are always the ones that can best get in touch with their feminine side. I don't expect to receive any pats on the back for saying that, but it is true nonetheless.

With this book, I set out to do two things:

- First, to write a biography that is also a cultural history of jazz. Miles Davis once asked me to stop using the term "jazz" to describe his music. He said he preferred that I say "social music" instead. His point was that the music we call jazz is a form of expression that is rooted deeply in southern culture. Jazz was a word that "outsiders" used to describe that music. Of course, I did not agree to stop using the word "jazz" for obvious reasons, but I have written this book with Davis's essential viewpoint in mind since it is one with which I happen to agree.

- Second, to set the record straight on Lil Hardin Armstrong: not only was she the cofounder of jazz and a prolific songwriter, she was a role model for how to live life as a musician and entertainer. She was a visionary with a heart of gold. I can think of no one in music, male or female, that I respect more.

It is my belief that Lil is the most important woman in jazz history. If you made a list of individuals who contributed the most to jazz, Louis Armstrong and Duke Ellington would occupy the top two spots; but Lil, I think, would belong in the third spot. I say that not because of her skills as a pianist—she was energetic, but, frankly, not a virtuoso performer—but because of her contributions as a songwriter, recording artist, and behind-the-scenes player in the creation of what later became known as jazz.

Louis Armstrong was a genius, probably the most talented individual to ever play a musical instrument. But I think it is doubtful that genius would have emerged to the degree it did were it not for the efforts of Lil. In any given year, there are millions of talented musicians in the United States. Hundreds may qualify as geniuses, but few are successful because they lack the skills to translate their genius into financial and artistic success.

That is what Lil did for Louis: she showed him how to present himself and their music to the world in a way that ensured his success. If she got lost in the process, it was a price she was willing to pay. That does not mean that we should allow the injustice to continue.

The Memphis Blues

At the turn of the nineteenth century, Memphis, Tennessee, was a bleak and foreboding place in which to live, especially for African Americans. The Civil War had been over for thirty-five years, but a series of catastrophic events had sent Memphis reeling, socially and economically. By 1900 it was a city against the ropes, though there were faint rays of hope that occasionally penetrated the ever-gray skyline.

When a U.S. Census worker visited the William and Dempsey Hardin household on June 6, 1900, there were three adult males living in the duplex at 206 Broadway Street—William, who was thirty-five; Abraham Martin, William's twenty-three-year-old brother-in-law; and Stewart Herbert, a twenty-year-old boarder—but only Abraham reported income to the census worker.

William told the census worker that he was a day laborer who had not worked in twelve months. Herbert said he had not worked in five months. That may or may not have been true. Southerners of that era, white and black, were not in the habit of providing

1

intimate financial information to representatives of the federal government, regardless of whether or not they spoke with a friendly accent. Despite his statement to the census worker, it is doubtful that Herbert would have been allowed to remain in the Hardin household without making a financial contribution.

Also in the household were Dempsey, William's twenty-five-year-old wife, their two-year-old daughter, Lillian Beatrice (affectionately known as Lil), Dempsey's fifty-year-old mother Priscilla Martin, and two of Priscilla's thirteen children—Mandy Martin, twenty-seven, and John, four years of age. Of that eight-person household, only Dempsey could read and write.

Lil was not Dempsey's only child—another child had died before Lil was born—but she was raised as if she were an only child. She was doted over by her mother and treated as if she were someone special. Certainly, Dempsey wanted things for her daughter that she never had. She was ambitious without being confrontational, and she was a dreamer who never lost sight of the limitations imposed by white society.

In 1900, most of the African Americans in Memphis lived in segregated neighborhood pockets that bordered the southern rim of the city. Most lived in neighborhoods located south of the downtown area, but smaller black neighborhoods stretched out around midtown and into east Memphis, where most of the city's white residents lived. Those "safer" black neighborhoods were allowed to prosper in white areas of the city so that black domestic workers could come and go with relative ease. They were considered better neighborhoods in which to raise children because they were across town from the crime-infested downtown district.

The neighborhood where the Hardins lived was in the densely populated section south of downtown. They lived one block east of Kentucky Street, which ran north to south from the downtown area. It was a residential area, but close enough to the predominantly black Beale Street entertainment district to make the family-oriented Dempseys uncomfortable.

For most of her life, Dempsey worked as a cook in white households. As far as jobs went, that was about as good as it could get for a black woman with a family, for it offered not only a steady income but various perks such as discarded clothing and household furnishings. Often it was the equivalent of being adopted by a white family. Dempsey didn't like the system, but she knew how to work it to her benefit.

By 1900, not much had changed in Memphis over the preceding one hundred years. Prior to the Civil War, the city was a bustling slave trade center, and with good reason: in the decades leading up to the war, Memphis was the largest inland cotton-trading center in the world. Nearly half a million bales of cotton were shipped through the city each year, representing a fifty-million-dollar-a-year economy that gave Memphis the same degree of national economic clout that computer-rich cities such as Seattle had throughout the 1990s.

The reason for the city's success as a trading center was entirely geographical. Located on a series of bluffs that towered fifty to one hundred feet above the Mississippi River, it was largely immune to the annual flooding that accompanied the river and devastated other cities in lower-lying areas. Slaves were imported from western Africa and transported to New Orleans, where they were then taken by riverboat to Memphis, where they were sold and re-sold to plantation owners throughout Mississippi, Arkansas, northwestern Alabama, and northeastern Louisiana.

One by-product of the city's status as a slave port was a large African-American population. In the 1830s, approximately one-third of southwest Tennessee's population was composed of slaves and by 1840 the percentage had increased to 40 percent.[1] For the next one hundred and fifty years, the city's African

American population hovered near 50 percent, not exceeding that until the early 1990s, when, for the first time, the African-American population broke the 50-percent barrier, establishing a racial majority that resulted in the election of the city's first African-American mayor.

For Lil, slavery was not an abstraction. She grew up in a household with a former slave—her grandmother, Priscilla Martin. Although still relatively young at fifty when the census worker visited in 1900, Priscilla had been born into slavery in 1850 in Lafayette County near Oxford, Mississippi, about eighty miles southeast of Memphis. Her name then was Priscilla Thompson.

Nobel Prize–winning author William Faulkner wrote extensively about the culture into which Priscilla was born and, considering the small population of the area surrounding Oxford, there is a great likelihood that the two families had more than a passing acquaintance with each other.

For Priscilla, Yoknapatawpha County, Faulkner's "postage stamp" of fictional territory that combined elements of life in Lafayette County and nearby Tippah County, was no fantasy representation—it was the reality of her daily existence. Indeed, since it was customary for slaves to take the surnames of their owners, it is possible that she once belonged to John Wesley Thompson, a Faulkner in-law whom biographer Joseph Blotner has described as a "strong and sometimes violent man, a fitting father-surrogate for the model for Colonel John Sartoris."[2] Shortly before Priscilla was born, Thompson was named the district attorney for the judicial district in which she lived.

Priscilla was eleven years of age in 1861 when Mississippi seceded from the Union to fight with the Confederacy. By the time she was fifteen, she had witnessed the excitement and the despair, the boom times and the hardships, the violence and the tenderness, and the unforgiving poverty that the Civil War brought to the Oxford area.

Priscilla was there when General Ulysses S. Grant captured the Lafayette County courthouse in Oxford, surrounding it with the tents of an Illinois regiment, and she was there in 1964 when federal troops set fire to the courthouse and several Oxford residences. "Where once stood a handsome little country town," wrote an Illinois correspondent about the fire, "now only remain the blackened skeletons of houses, and smoldering ruins."[3]

By the end of the war, Oxford and Lafayette County were in a shambles, as was most of the South. Of the seventy-eight thousand Mississippians who went off to war, more than fifty-nine thousand were killed or wounded. During the first year of peace, Mississippi allocated one-fifth of its total revenues to purchase artificial arms and legs for returning soldiers.

Under the terms of Reconstruction, the federal government prohibited Confederate veterans from voting or running for elective office. Since women were more than half a century away from achieving voting rights, that meant that the voting pool was comprised of white males who never served in the Confederacy, so-called carpetbaggers from the North, and black males who went directly from slavery into the voting booth.

The final months of the Civil War were a nightmare for southern civilians, white and black. U.S. Army troops burned, looted, and killed across a wide section of the South. After the war, it only got worse. The defeated states were divided up into military districts, and troops were stationed in towns across the South. The Freedman Bureau was created to oversee the emancipation of the freed slaves.

Southerners thus became the only Americans, other than indigenous Native Americans, to ever live as a defeated nation under military rule. It is not the sort of experience that quickly dissipates from a people's collective consciousness. But that is only part of the story. Former officers of the Confederate army, using much the same military techniques employed by the U.S. Army, burned, looted, and killed families of newly freed slaves under the banner of the Ku Klux Klan, creating a wave of terror across the South. Freedman Bureau records show that more than one thousand blacks were murdered in Texas by whites during the first three years of Reconstruction.

Immediately after the war, Republicans in northern states moved to the South to take advantage of the changing economic situation. They bought burned out plantations and farms from widows who had no male family members left to work the land. Some hired freed slaves and attempted to adapt them to northern, industrial-type schedules of work, only to discover that Southerners, white and black, liked to work at their own pace.

Politically, the Republicans and the freed slaves made strong showings in elections and constitutional conventions across the South. In the first presidential election held after the war, Republican Ulysses S. Grant carried Mississippi by a margin of two to one. In 1875 Mississippi elected a black lieutenant governor, and from 1869 to 1878 the office of secretary of state in Mississippi was held exclusively by freed slaves.

Ironically, the two groups that had the least involvement in the Civil War—white civilians and freed slaves—suffered the most at the war's end and continued to do so throughout Reconstruction. Technically, Reconstruction lasted from 1867 to 1877, but in reality it continued until 1890 and even beyond in some states.

There's an old southern saying that when "Mama ain't happy, ain't nobody happy." The same sentiment applied to white landowners after the war: when they were unhappy, everyone in the community was unhappy—and that included hundreds of ex-slaves in and around Oxford who comprised about 40 percent of the population.

Slaves who had been sold for between eight hundred and fifteen hundred dollars each suddenly found themselves without homes or jobs or any objective measure of their worth. If the war had been fought over slavery, as they were told, why were federal troops so hard on them during Reconstruction?

In the spring and early summer of 1865, the U.S. Army forbade freed slaves to travel without passes from their employers. They also were prohibited from being on the streets at night and prohibited from engaging in "insubordination," which is to say they could still go to jail for talking back to white employers. In 1865, Mississippi and South Carolina enacted the first "Black Codes," which required all blacks to possess written evidence of guaranteed employment for the upcoming year. If they violated their work contracts, any white citizen could arrest them.

Under slavery, women were responsible for the care of the family unit. One of the first things that happened to black families after the emancipation was the emergence of a patriarchal system. Black men insisted on controlling the economic destinies of their families. Women and children were removed from the rigors of farm labor and sent home. Women were encouraged to submit to the authority of their husbands and become dutiful homemakers. Children were encouraged to go to school.

At first, women welcomed the break from hard labor in the fields. But as time went by, it quickly became apparent that it would be impossible for most families to exist on the meager earnings of one wage earner. Gradually, the women returned to work, sometimes in the fields, but most often as household domestics. Even that was not usually enough. School terms were altered so that black children could work in the fields during the planting and harvesting seasons. The optimism of emancipation quickly turned to despair as black families found themselves immersed in slavery of a different sort.

One of the first reactions among blacks to emancipation was flight from the rural areas of the South into the cities, where it was felt they would have more opportunities. As it turned out, few jobs were available for freed slaves. Tensions ran high as blacks struggled with great expectations and whites struggled with the rapidly changing demographics of the cities.

Violence was commonplace. In Memphis, for example, there was a race riot in 1868 that left forty-six blacks and two whites dead. The riot was instigated by a traffic accident in which a cart driven by a black man collided with a wagon driven by a white man. So-called right of way battles became commonplace as freed slaves struggled to balance the promise of freedom with the reality of everyday life.

One social result of the exodus was racial segregation. On the plantations, whites and blacks lived in close proximity. Although the social status of the slaves and the landowners remained at polar opposites, there was nonetheless a high degree of integration on the plantations. Each race was able to observe the other within the context of daily living. Not so in the cities, where freed slaves lived in squalid shantytowns in segregated neighborhoods. Daily conversations with whites became a rarity. As social contact between the races decreased, suspicions, fears, and hostility increased.

During slavery, blacks were prohibited from marrying. They were allowed to form marital unions, of course, and they could even ask ministers to bless those unions, but legal marriages were out of the question. After emancipation, many freed slaves rushed to the courthouses to legalize their marital unions, but just as many did not, for fear of offending angry whites in the courthouse.

For five years after the war, there was a lot of confusion in Mississippi. Although federal troops were in place to enforce emancipation, there was uncertainty among the state's residents, white and black, over the state's failure to adopt a new constitution and ratify the fifteenth amendment to give African Americans the right to vote—and, without those actions, Mississippi was blocked from being readmitted to the union.

For those five years Mississippi was neither a state nor an independent territory. It was a defeated nation living under military rule, governed by military officers based in the Fourth Military District in Memphis. After years of political wrangling, Mississippi voters approved a new constitution and ratified the fifteenth amendment in July 1869, an action that led to statewide elections in November and December. Elected to the posts of U.S. Senator were General Adelbert Ames, Mississippi's then military governor, and a black man named Hiram Revels.[4]

On February 12, 1870, just eleven days before Mississippi was readmitted to the Union by the U.S. Senate, Priscilla Thompson and Taylor Martin went into the Lafayette Country courthouse, the same building that had been burned by federal troops, to obtain a marriage license. That record is still in existence, although it has been tattered somewhat by the passage of time. Later that same day they were married by a minister named Austin Slate. Not much is known about Taylor Martin. During a 2000 visit to Lafayette County, local residents told the author that the Martin family had lived for generations in the small community of Taylor, located a few miles southwest of Oxford. It is not unreasonable to assume that a former slave by the name of Taylor Martin would have originated in Taylor.

One way to understand what life was like for Lil's mother and father is to read Faulkner's accounts of race relations in that era, for no one has ever written a more detailed and compassionate history of the South for those times. Sometimes fiction can come closer to the truth than even the most determined scholarship. Faulkner was especially insightful when writing about the conflicting emotions former slaves felt during Reconstruction. In *The Unvanquished*, Granny Millard chastises former slave Loosh for leaving the plantation after the emancipation. "I going," he said. "I done been freed; God's own angel proclaimed me free and gonter general me to Jordan. I don't belong to John Sartoris now; I belong to me and God." His wife Philadelphy feels differently. "Fore God, Miss Rosa," she said. "I tried to stop him. I done tried."[5]

There is no record of when Priscilla and Taylor Martin moved to Memphis, but it obviously took place sometime between 1870 and 1898, most likely in the 1880s. In many ways, that was one of the most enlightening and terrifying periods in the city's history. Enlightening, because Reconstruction opened up the political process to blacks for the first time: during those years, African Americans rose to positions of authority as market master and wharf master and were appointed or elected to the city board of education, county registrar, the police department, and the county court.[6] Terrifying, because of a series of yellow fever epidemics: between 1803 and 1900, there were nearly forty outbreaks of the mosquito-spread disease. The outbreak in 1853 alone killed more than eleven thousand Memphians. In 1878, another outbreak resulted in the exodus of an estimated twenty-five thousand residents as they fled to the countryside.

In a display of unprecedented heroism, most of the city's black residents stayed put during the epidemic, supplying the majority of the three thousand nurses who cared for the sick and dying. So many whites fled that the remaining blacks comprised about 70 percent of the total population. Of the six thousand whites who remained, virtually all were stricken by the fever, resulting in the deaths of about two-thirds of them. Incredibly, of the fourteen thousand blacks that remained, less than one thousand died of the disease, giving credence to the long-held belief among some Southerners that if Jews were the chosen people in the Middle East, African Americans were the chosen ones in America.

Taylor and Priscilla had thirteen children, seven of whom died prior to 1900. It is clear that Taylor, whether because of death or separation, was no longer a part of Priscilla's life when the census worker arrived at the Hardin household in June 1900.

William Hardin, Lil's father, is an enigma. Little is known about him except that he was a Civil War baby boomer, born in January 1865. In 1895, at the age of thirty, he married Dempsey. It was an advanced age for marriage and probably means that he had previous domestic relationships. At that time, Southerners, black and white, tended to pair off well before their eighteenth birthday.

Later in life, Lil told interviewers that her father died when she was two, which, if true, meant that he died shortly after the census worker visited in 1900. She also told interviewers that her father worked for the railroad. Apparently, neither of those statements was true. Death records for Memphis and Shelby County—and northern Mississippi—reveal no mention of William Hardin's death. (When it came to her early years, Lil sometimes displayed a propensity for bending the truth. Although she was born in 1898, she repeatedly told interviewers throughout her life that she was born in 1900.)

Was it possible that William passed away in some other jurisdiction while working for the railroad? Not if he was being truthful when he told the census worker that he was an unemployed day laborer. Most likely he abandoned his family, as Priscilla's husband Taylor probably did, and found a new life somewhere else. The Memphis city directory shows an African American by the name of William Hardin living in a separate residence from Dempsey in 1903 and at a rooming house in 1905.

Evidence that William left the household before 1902 is strong, for that was the year that Dempsey and Lil moved into a boarding house at 196 Broadway, just a few doors down from their duplex apartment. William dropped out of sight, as did Priscilla and her children. Lil grew up in a matriarchal household that still resonated with stories about slavery. It would affect her decision-making for the remainder of her life.

By the time Lil was ten, Memphis was an exciting place to live. Just a few blocks away from her boarding house was Beale Street, by then one of the most infamous gathering places in the nation for blacks. The street was only about three blocks in length, but it was packed with nightclubs, pawnshops, whorehouses, clothing stores, drugstores, and restaurants. It was a place where a visitor could buy a drink, eat a hearty meal of tamales or turnip greens and ham, listen to some of the best blues in the world, purchase a small box of cocaine from one of the drug stores, and tumble with the prostitute of his choice—all for under one dollar. Of course, there was no shortage of Memphians who felt that all of the above, with the exception of the tamales and turnip greens and ham, were an abomination that would lead its supporters straight to hell.

Several blocks east of Lil's boarding house, on Jennette Street, was the home of W. C. Handy, the man many consider the father of the blues. He moved to Memphis from Mississippi in 1905 at the age of thirty-two, lured there by the bright lights of the city and its thriving music scene. In Mississippi, he had formed a band that played for social functions and political gatherings. In Memphis, he did much the same thing, booking his new band at barbecues and political rallies.

Sometimes he and his band simply marched up and down the streets around Beale Street. Truthfully, the band didn't march so much as it sauntered. Although the band played some military marches, as was the custom at that time, it mostly played polkas, waltzes, and one-steps, musical styles that hardly lent themselves to rigid march formations . . . so they strolled while they played, New Orleans style, creating a festive atmosphere that drew adults and children alike out into the streets.

Among the youngsters lured out into the street was Alberta Hunter, who was ten years of age when Handy first moved to Memphis. She and her mother lived in a rented room at 170 Beale. Alberta's father abandoned the family when she was very young and her mother worked as a chambermaid in a whorehouse to support the family.

Hunter literally grew up in the heart of the entertainment district. In later years, she recalled with great fondness the way Handy and his band, dressed in colorful uniforms, strutted up and down the street outside her rooming house: "We'd hear that ta-da, ta-da of the band, and Lord, we'd be out the door so fast."[7]

Even so, Hunter always denied ever working on Beale Street. "I always wanted to stay away from anything that had a reputation of being bad," she said, adding that any woman who sang on the street was considered to be a bad person. If that had been her only chance to start a singing career, she explained, "I'd rather not have the chance."

In 1911, at the age of sixteen, Hunter boarded a train and went to Chicago to live with the daughter of her mother's friend. Although it was there that she began her illustrious career as one of the nation's premier blues singers, she never forgot the early thrills and musical influences she experienced in Memphis.

Joining Lil and Alberta in Memphis, though after 1910, was renowned guitarist and singer Memphis Minnie, who was born in Louisiana but moved to north Mississippi at an early age. By the time she was a teen, she was a frequent visitor to Beale Street, almost certainly without her family's permission.

She learned to play guitar while in her teens and later became one of the most accomplished guitarists in blues history, but in the beginning she was more interested in the party atmosphere on Beale than in any particular type of music. A big part of that had to do with booze, cocaine, and raucous music of the type that inspired fear in the hearts of mothers of both races. Those who worked with Minnie in later years maintained that she was more than an observer to the pay-as-you-go sexuality on Beale: they said she worked as a prostitute, not just in her early years, but well into her career. Many of the songs she penned reflected that experience.

There has never been any evidence that Lil, Alberta, and Minnie ever knew each other as youngsters, but the thought of the three of them traveling the same sidewalks and streets and sharing similar experiences is interesting to ponder. Alberta did run into Lil later, once she moved to Chicago, at which time they had plenty to talk about. Alberta was always horrified by the blatant sexuality that was such a big part of Beale Street's reputation, but her disapproval may have been due to the fact that she was a lesbian. Beale was about as heterosexual as you can get, and that may have offended Alberta's emerging sensibilities as a gay woman.

Actually, Beale Street welcomed women of all sexual preferences and had a reputation as being the best place in the nation for female musicians to work. Women were protected because of their moneymaking potential and valued because of their skills, whether musical or sexual. If there was ever a geographical location that placed female musicians on a pedestal, it was Beale Street.

Crime was the only downside to the gaiety. The Memphis murder rate was so high that the Prudential Insurance Company labeled the city the "murder capital" of the nation. Cocaine addiction was so rampant that the city had to establish programs to combat its devastating effect. Muggings, robberies, and assaults were commonplace, primarily because of the cocaine and morphine problem and the large number of prostitutes in the city.

Recovery from the addictive effects of drugs often involved public penitence, assuming all the characteristics of a religious testimony and conversion. In the January 11, 1903, edition of the *Memphis Morning News*, Mrs. Anis Garritt gave a ringing endorsement of her recovery from morphine addiction in the city-sponsored Old Homestead treatment center. "When I entered the Old Homestead for the treatment of the drug habit, I was almost a dead woman," she wrote. "But after a three week course of treatment I returned home, not only cured of the drug habit but greatly improved mentally and physically, and it is a horrible thought to me now, when I think that I once was a slave of morphine and that it took an ounce of morphine a week to keep me from suffering."

To deal with the large number of young girls flooding into Memphis from Mississippi and Arkansas to become prostitutes, the city established a Women's Protection Bureau. By 1923, the bureau was handling the cases of eleven hundred women per year. There are no existing records on the racial status of the prostitutes who inhabited the city, but there is anecdotal evidence that a large number of them were young white girls who were lured to the city by dreams of financial success. Although the whorehouses offered former slaves and the sons of slaves opportunities for sexual encounters with white women, there was a drawback—they were asked by the madams to wait until after all the white customers had their fill.

Crimes traditionally received prominent display in the morning newspaper, *The Commercial Appeal*. In 1905, the newspaper heralded the New Year with a front-page story about a "Negro Demon" that beat the head of his victim into an "unrecognizable mass." On February 3, 1902, the newspaper splashed on its front page a vicious robbery and murder of a saloonkeeper that took place on a street corner. The three men were apprehended in Illinois. The reporter convicted the men before they could even be returned to Memphis for trial. Reflecting the type of "yellow" journalism that was prevalent in the city, the reporter wrote: "A confession or any other form of direct proof would not add much strength in the chain of evidence which now coils about these men."

"Beale Street told macabre stories of its callousness to violence," wrote Margaret McKee and Fred Chisenhall in their book *Beale Black & Blue*, "about a man's getting killed at a crap game and the other players dragging his body under the table and playing on top of him; about a killing in a night spot when the owners threw the body out the window; about a dive that provided a chute to the undertaker's; about an undertaker who sat on a dead gambler's body until his hearse came, so that he would be sure to get the funeral."

Seemingly immune to all that was W. C. Handy, who proceeded to write innovative new music amid the violence and chaos that occurred each day—and then was revisited the following day by the newspaper in language designed to titillate. Handy did not invent the blues—since it sprang from a folk tradition that existed long before modern methods of documentation, the true "inventor" of the blues will never be known with certainty—but he was the first person to commit the blues to musical notation.

Handy's genius lay in his ability to blend the rhythmic country-folk music he heard in the Delta with classic European instrumentation in such a way as to create a new music that was neither American country-folk nor European. It was light-years ahead of the rustic, monatomic, chant-like music he heard in the Delta—he called it "primitive"—and it was more energetic and sophisticated than any of the popular music then in vogue.

Handy might never have risen above his status as a street and private party musician were it not for the arrival of a transplanted

Mississippian named E. H. Crump. Shortly after moving to Memphis in 1994 from Holly Springs, Mississippi, near Oxford, he got a job as a bookkeeper at a buggy business.

For Faulkner readers, Crump was cut from the same cloth as the white-trash Snopes family in *The Unvanquished* and *The Hamlet*. Of Flem Snopes, Faulkner wrote that he had "eyes the color of stagnant water, and projecting from among the other features in startling and sudden paradox, a tiny predatory nose like the beak of a small hawk." Had he added a description of a red shock of hair rising several inches above his brow, he might just as well have been describing Crump himself.

Within four years of arriving in Memphis, Crump was made an officer in the company. He soon married a Memphis socialite, whose family loaned him fifty thousand dollars to purchase the buggy business so that he and his new bride would have a stable financial future. Tall and garrulous, the affable redhead soon discovered he had a knack for dealing with people of different races and social backgrounds. He directed that talent toward politics, where he found success as a politician. In 1905, at the age of thirty-one, he won a seat on the city's lower legislative council. His involvement in politics happened to coincide with a reform sentiment among the white population.

Ever so often, white Memphians decided that Beale Street needed cleaning up. Saloons, gambling dins, and whorehouses were shut down and the city was proclaimed safe once again for children and virginal women. That sentiment was afoot in 1909 when Crump decided to run for mayor as a reform candidate. He looked at the voting pool and saw that there was a large segment of white voters who wanted Beale Street shut down and a large segment of black voters who wanted to maintain the status quo. The swing votes, as he figured it, lay with black voters like Dempsey Hardin who thought that Beale Street was little more than a playground for Satan himself.[8]

Crump knew how to get the white votes he needed. What he didn't know was how to get the black votes. To bridge that gap, his campaign organization sought out the most likable and well-regarded musician on Beale Street—W. C. Handy. They asked him to write a campaign song for the candidate, one that would put smiles on the faces of white voters and inspire confidence among those black voters who favored reform.

While Handy had performed for all sorts of white political gatherings in Mississippi, he and his nine-piece band played the popular music of the day in Memphis, nothing original or controversial. At first, Handy was stumped by the assignment. What he needed was an original idea, one that would appeal to both whites and blacks.

The idea that kept returning to him was one that was inspired by something that happened at one of his performances in Mississippi. During a break, he was asked if three local musicians, all raggedly dressed black men, could perform a few songs of their own. Handy agreed, though reluctantly, but once they took the stage he was amazed at the way in which the white audience greeted them.

"A rain of silver dollars began to fall" from the white audience, he wrote in his autobiography. "The boys lay more money than my nine musicians were being paid for the entire engagement." It was then, he explained, that he understood "the beauty of primitive music."

At that time, popular music was written in sixteen-bar segments. To create his campaign song, Handy appropriated the twelve-bar, three-line structure of the folk blues and added a bass line in a tango rhythm and a three-chord harmonic structure. When it was completed he had a song with African rhythms and European instrumentation. He appropriately titled the song "Mister Crump."

With lyrics that promised nothing but good times ahead with a Crump victory and feel-good music that seemed to celebrate life itself, the song was an instant hit, winning the approval of both whites and blacks. Crump won the election by a mere seventy-nine votes and went on to build a political machine that lasted for nearly half a century.

Once the election was over, Handy wrote new lyrics for the song, using words that poked fun at Crump's ideas of reform. "Luckily for us, Mr. Crump himself didn't hear us sing these [new] words," Handy wrote in his autobiography.

Encouraged by reaction to "Mister Crump," Handy changed the title to "The Memphis Blues." When he offered the song to New York publishers, they all turned it down. Three years later, he asked the manager of a Memphis music store if he would help him get the song published. The manager told him he couldn't do that, but would be happy to sell the music in the store if Handy paid to have it printed.

In 1912, Handy's self-published version of "The Memphis Blues" went on sale in the music store. Since he was unable to get the other stores in town to sell the music, Handy never recouped his investment in the sheet music. When the one store that sold the music offered to reimburse Handy for the printing costs in exchange for the copyright to the song, he readily agreed. With a wife and four children at home, he needed the money and felt he had little choice.[9]

As it turned out, "The Memphis Blues" was a tremendous hit, its success spreading first to New Orleans, then to Chicago and on to New York. Handy wrote many other successful songs— "The St. Louis Blues," "The Beale Street Blues," and "Joe Turner Blues," to name a few—but he never profited financially from the initial success of the song that many consider the first-ever blues composition. Twenty-eight years after the copyright expired, the song reverted back to Handy and he eventually made money from it; but the bitterness of the transaction stayed with him for a long time.

As exciting and important as Handy's success appeared to succeeding generations, it was not greeted with universal approval in the black Memphis community. Dempsey Hardin was an ardent music fan—indeed she considered herself a proficient soprano—but she considered blues and jazz to be the devil's music. Sacred music was of greater interest to her, and that was the direction she encouraged Lil to take.

In later years, Lil told of how she began playing the organ at an early age in the living room of their house, citing that as a reason why her mother decided to enroll her in music lessons at the age of six. Since they lived in a rooming house, it is unlikely the organ belonged to them. More likely, it was in the common living area of the boarding house. At any rate, Lil had fond memories of playing the organ with her younger cousin. When Lil played the organ the cousin pumped the pedals, and when the cousin played Lil took over operation of the pedals.

Lil's music instructor was actually one of her schoolteachers. The lessons were scheduled in the afternoons after school. "Now that I've studied so much afterward, I know she wasn't so good to begin with," Lil later recalled. "Anyway, she taught me how to read the notes."[10]

By the time Lil was nine, she was good enough to be the organist for her Sunday school class at the Lebanon Baptist Church. Her favorite hymn was "Onward Christian Soldiers," but she didn't play it the way everyone else did. She added a little something extra. The other children loved to sing along with her, but it was that extra pizzazz in her music that caused the pastor to peer over his eyeglasses at Lil with a disapproving stare.

Years later, she realized that the something "extra" in her music was a touch of blues, but at the age of nine she was not yet aware of blues. The only time she ever heard the word was when Priscilla used it in a disparaging way. Once she was on the back porch with a cousin who played guitar. When Priscilla heard the music she ran out onto the porch and shooed Lil away, proclaiming it to be vulgar music of the worst sort.

More to Dempsey's liking was the music advocated by Mrs. Hicks' School of Music, where Lil received piano lessons. At commencement, sixteen-year-old Lil was paired off with the yearlong top student in a contest to determine a winner. "Lil was determined to outdo her rival, but near the end of her performance, she lost her place," reports author Laurence Bergreen. "She had the presence of mind to improvise her way to the end. The feat only made her seem more talented, and she was declared the winner on the spot."

In later years, she would refer back to that day as the first indication she had that there was something inside her that set her apart. She liked to refer to herself as a child prodigy, but, of course, she was midway through her teen years when the contest occurred. This tendency to represent herself as a child is one that lasted for many years. She was immature as a teen and young adult, and she sometimes described herself as being "pushy" and "assertive."

In early 1915, Dempsey began exploring alternatives for Lil's education. She had always felt that there was something special about her only child, something that could be developed and, who knows, perhaps enable her to rise high within the church.

Working as a family cook, Dempsey was exposed on a daily basis to the sons and daughters of her white employers. They were no brighter, no more talented than her darling Lil, yet their futures never seemed in doubt. They would all be educated, marry well, and live good lives—or so it seemed to Dempsey.

Fragmented by violence, corrupt politics, strained race relations, drug addiction, teen pregnancies, an antieducational mindset, and a stagnant economy, Memphis was no place to raise a high-spirited teenage girl. What Dempsey feared most was that Lil's strength—her passion for music—would lead her to Beale Street and a life of prostitution. With so few opportunities for African Americans in Memphis, Dempsey looked elsewhere. She was committed to doing whatever it took to give Lil the start in life that she never had, indeed that no one in her family had ever had.

Fisk University in Nashville seemed perfect. Founded in 1865 under the auspices of the American Missionary Association of New York City and the Western Freedman's Aid Commission of Cincinnati, it was dedicated to providing the sons and daughters of former slaves with a Christian education that was strong both spiritually and academically. The first classes were held in the barracks of a converted Union army hospital just outside Nashville.

Since money for the school was scarce in the beginning, school administrators gathered the abandoned handcuffs and chains from the city's slave quarters and sold them for scrap iron, earning enough to purchase spelling books and Bibles. Later, it became evident that contributions from trustees and fund-raising drives by students would not be enough to sustain the school.

Fisk treasurer and music teacher George L. White put together a group of students named the Jubilee Singers for a tour in the North in an effort to raise money for the school. In the beginning, their reception was uncertain and often confusing. Hotels accepted reservations for them thinking they were white singers who worked in black face. When they arrived, they were sometimes asked to leave the hotel.[11]

Only when they stopped singing "white" songs such as "Home, Sweet Home" and "There's Moonlight on the Lake" and began performing spirituals or "slave songs," as they were called at the time, did their popularity explode. The music was especially poignant because seven of the original nine men and women in the group had themselves been slaves. Shortly before they returned to Nashville, they performed at the White House for President Ulysses S. Grant, who made it a point to shake hands with each of them. When they arrived back on campus, they brought with them twenty thousand dollars, a considerable amount by 1860 standards.

For the next one hundred and forty years the Jubilee Singers remained a major public relations and fund-raising vehicle for the university. No one knows if Dempsey dreamed of Lil becoming a Jubilee Singer, but that was probably one of the reasons she was interested in Fisk, for the musical group was quite famous at the time and considered a role model for young African Americans.

The catalog Dempsey received from Fisk only confirmed her own instincts about the school. "The aim of the founders and supporters of Fisk University has always been to make its students strong, earnest, broadminded Christian men and women, who shall give their lives to the uplift of the people," said the catalog. "The distinctively religious services upon which attendance is required are a church service on Sunday morning, Sunday-school, chapel services on school days, and a midweek prayer meeting on Wednesday night." The school said it recognized the "absolute necessity" of structuring the right education for young women: "The highest interest of every community depends largely upon the intelligence, frugality, virtue, and noble aspirations of its women."

Dempsey must have said "Amen" to that all the way to the bank to withdraw her savings. Tuition costs, payable in advance, were thirteen dollars per semester, with room and board costing an additional fourteen dollars. Registration and other fees boosted the total cost to $36.50 per semester. That was a significant sum for a cook, but Dempsey had been saving her earnings and may have received help from one of her employers.

Lil was enrolled in the 1915-1916 school year, with registration taking place on September 18. It was a good time to leave Memphis. The newspapers were filled with disturbing news. Mayor Boss Crump was the target of a legal ouster by the state attorney general over the mayor's refusal to enforce Prohibition laws. Whereas he had originally campaigned on a reform platform that targeted Beale Street, he now risked ouster because he refused to shut down Beale Street. The difference in the two positions can be attributed to the fact that he now received campaign contributions from the saloonkeepers and bootleggers. The dispute only heightened the crisis atmosphere in the city.

The summer months in Memphis have always been strange, and the summer of 1915 was no exception. The week before Lil left for Fisk, the newspaper reported that an unidentified white man was found in a gutter off Beale, with a fractured skull and an "ugly" gash on the back of his head. A black youth was arrested for "insulting" a white woman. According to the news story, he entered a white woman's house on the pretense of delivering a note. In an effort to escape, he poured turpentine on his feet in the hopes that would throw the bloodhounds off the track.

Yet another story that week told of a juvenile court judge who ordered an unruly boy to wear a frilly dress as his punishment: "There is not a boy at the court who would not much rather take a sound thrashing than to be forced to sit around in plain view of everybody in an uncomfortable and embarrassing bit of strange feminine apparel," observed the newspaper. Then there was the story in the *Memphis Press Scimitar* about the two black men who were burned alive at the stake for killing a deputy sheriff.

Traveling the two hundred miles to Nashville was like entering a long tunnel and then emerging into the light of day. Memphis was predominantly black, with a history of gritty politics and organized crime; Nashville was predominantly white, with a history of political gentility and an aversion to organized crime.

More than once Memphis discussed seceding from Tennessee to form a separate state, one more attuned to the politics and lifestyles of Mississippi; more than once, Nashvillians prayed that Memphis would take that step and rid them of what they perceived to be a canker sore on its body politic.

It was against that backdrop that Dempsey sent Lil to the Promised Land, where young black girls grow up strong and independent and learn to march in step with the Lord's Drummer. She wanted Lil to become a lady, and no sacrifice on her part was too great if it resulted in that goal being realized.

Getting Lil's clothing together was no small matter since it meant assembling a wardrobe that conformed to the school's stringent uniform code. Required were: a white linen suit, with the waistcoat made from Butterwick pattern 8160 or McCall pattern 6495 (a minimum of three were needed); a navy blue suit, consisting of a coat, skirt, and Windsor tie, all of which were required to be purchased from the university at a cost of nearly sixteen dollars; and a special hat that was sold by the school at a "reasonable" price. "Uniform dress is required for church, Sunday school, Sunday dinner, calls, socials, and Friday night entertainment," advised the catalog. "Girls wearing mourning are not exempt from the uniform requirements."

Once Lil recovered from the decidedly un-Memphis dress code, she was subjected to a set of rules that must have made her cringe. According to the 1915 rulebook, the following were forbidden: "profanity, betting and gambling, the use of ardent spirits as a beverage, and the use of tobacco; also dancing between the sexes in the university or in public places. Promiscuous dancing and card playing during the school year are strongly disapproved of. No student is allowed to keep or use pistols or other weapons, or any fireworks, gasoline, or benzene . . . any student marrying during his course of study thereby severs his connection with the institution." Another regulation that was enforced but not mentioned in the guidebook was the school's requirement that male and female students always walk on opposite sides of the street and refrain from any eye contact.

Female students at the university were all expected to stay in Jubilee Hall, the first building erected on campus using the money raised by the singers. The building was situated on eight acres of land and surrounded with trees and shrubbery. Downtown Nashville was only one and one-half miles away, and transportation was available on a streetcar that passed near the school.

From a racial standpoint, Nashville had numerous advantages over Memphis. The area surrounding Fisk contained black middle-class neighborhoods that tended to act as a buffer between the university and segregated white neighbors, although in those years Nashville was never entirely segregated. In Memphis, black domestics lived in shantytowns or in downtown ghettos and commuted to their place of employment. In Nashville, black domestics often lived in the homes with their employers or in housing adjacent to their employers. The degree of equality was no higher in Nashville, but integration per se was more prevalent, at least on a surface level.

We may never know how well Lil adjusted to life on campus. In later years, she spoke infrequently of her time at Fisk. She sometimes told interviewers that she had graduated from the university, implying that she had obtained a university degree. At times she even displayed a degree tacked above the piano at her home.

Actually, Lil did not enroll in a university course of study and never received a degree. She was in a college preparatory program that offered high school courses chosen to prepare students for entry into the university. She was one of sixty-five students in the senior preparatory class. Only three other students in her program were from Memphis—two males and a female—with some students coming from as far away as Massachusetts and Ohio.

Lil took a variety of courses at Fisk. Among the required courses were English, science, Latin, and home economics. Music courses were not listed among those made available to students in the preparatory course program, but that does not necessarily mean that Lil was not allowed to enroll in specific courses. Since the financial well-being of the school was dependent on the continuing success of the Jubilee Singers, it is hard to imagine administrators blocking preparatory students from participating in music at some level at the university. The school needed all the talent it could find.

The music department had twenty pianos, including three concert grands, a pedal piano, three cabinet organs, and one pipe organ. The sheet music library consisted of more than four thousand titles, but it was not made available to students without fee. The piano instruction was very rigid in its expectations, and it is interesting to visualize Lil, as incorrigible as she could be at times, submitting to the instructor's authority.

The program consisted of eight "grades" through which students were expected to proceed, step by step. "Each grade consists of suitable studies and exercises, progressively arranged in difficulty of technique and interpretation," said the school catalog. "These pieces are selected from the works of the best composers. In order to pass from one grade to the next the student must practice faithfully and intelligently the exercises designed to give control to the fingers, hands and arms and to develop freedom and discrimination in the use of various kinds of touch."

If Lil was unhappy about all the rigid rules that were enforced at Fisk, she was certainly not alone. Shortly before her arrival at the school in 1915, a new president was appointed. Fayette Avery McKenzie was a white educator who had an almost obsessive belief in the value of rigid rules and regulations. That didn't go over too well with the students and alumni, but since he was adroit at raising funds from the white community, the university's board of trustees, most of whom were white, stuck with him. Students complained bitterly about the rules during Lil's stay at the university, but it was not until 1925 that they organized a strike that resulted in McKenzie's resignation.

In June 1916, Lil returned to Memphis. Her first week back, she was greeted by constant thunderstorms and unusually cool weather—and by a city that was seemingly bursting at the seams with World War I patriotism. More than twenty-five thousand residents turned out in the street for a parade that the morning newspaper called "the greatest patriotic demonstration ever held in the South."

"Twelve of the best bands in this section of the country have been engaged," reported the newspaper. "Also there will be a number of drum and fife corps in the line of march, and here and there will be noticed costumed drummers and fifers dressed as 'The Spirit of '76.'" If Lil did not attend the parade, she certainly would have heard it at the boarding house where Dempsey lived, for the acoustics of downtown Memphis were such that the boom-boom-boom of the parade would have carried up and down the streets of Lil's neighborhood with an urgency that would have been impossible to ignore.

Despite the magnitude of the celebration, the newspapers that week were filled with stories of violence and racial discord. Two black men were shot by police during the robbery of a wholesale liquor company located just off Beale. Police said they caught the men in the act of carrying liquor cases from the building. Another story that made big headlines was about an African-American man who got into a fight with the owner of a Greek restaurant over a bowl of soup. When the black man complained that the soup was cold, the restaurant owner refused to take it back to the cook. The fight broke out after the black man inverted the soup on the restaurant owner's head. Such was the stuff of which racially exploitive headlines were made.

For the next twelve months, Lil's life is an historical blur. She did not return to Fisk to complete her studies and what she did in Memphis during that time remains a mystery. The year after her return, Dempsey allowed her to buy sheet music. One of her first purchases was "They Made It Twice As Nice As Paradise and Called It Dixieland."

Once Lil learned to play it, she then purchased "Alexander's Ragtime Band," committing it to memory. Even though she hated any form of popular music, Dempsey loosened up with time, allowing Lil to select her own music. Then one day, Lil brought home the sheet music for "St. Louis Blues."

When Dempsey found it in Lil's room, she did what any concerned mother of that era would have done: she beat the "devil" out of Lil with a broomstick.

Satan's music was the final straw. In 1917 Lil and Dempsey packed up all their transportable belongings and said goodbye to Memphis, a city bluesman Sleepy John Estes once called "the center of all evil in the known universe."

Lil Finds a Home in Chicago

At one time, the *City of New Orleans* was the pride of the Illinois Central railroad. Its overnight run from New Orleans to Chicago was the stuff of which dreams—and songs—were made. More than once it was celebrated in music, most recently with Steve Goodman's 1970s anthem, "City of New Orleans," whose chorus of "Good Morning, America, how are you?" symbolizes the infectious optimism that has characterized passengers on that rail line for generations.

If you lived in Memphis in 1917, the *City of New Orleans* was the only reliable way to travel to Chicago. Dempsey and Lil most likely rode the train when they packed up all their belongings and said goodbye to Memphis. What they found when they arrived in Chicago was a city not entirely unlike the one they had left behind.

Like Memphis, Chicago grappled with its public sense of decency. In 1918, there was a great debate over an Albin Polaskey statue named "The Sower," which had been erected on the steps of the Art Institute. Although the statue had stood outside public buildings in Buffalo, New York, and San Francisco without incident, Chicago residents were offended by its nudity and complained to the police. Accordingly, the Institute was given twenty-four hours to move the statue inside, under penalty of arrest.[1]

Like Memphis, Chicago struggled with problems related to race relations. Dempsey and Lil were among 454,000 African Americans who migrated from the South between 1910 and 1920. Chicago saw its black population grow from 44,103 to 277,731 between the years of 1910 and 1940.[2] By the time Dempsey and Lil arrived, there were about 125,000 blacks living in the city.

Most of the blacks who moved to Chicago during this period congregated in neighborhoods south of the Illinois Central terminal. There on the South side they built an entertainment district named the "Stroll," a collection of nightclubs that bore a striking resemblance to Beale Street. With its bright lights and gritty nightclubs, prostitutes and gambling dins, the Stroll soon gained a nationwide reputation among African Americans. Whites, too, patronized the nightclubs known as "black-and-tans," where the police allowed racial mixing.

Race relations in Chicago were generally better than they were in Memphis, but that was not always the case. Newspapers of the era are filled with accounts of racial abuse, though, unlike Memphis, there was a public debate about how to improve race relations. A page-one *Chicago Tribune* headline in 1919 read: "Robertson and Merriam Debate For Negro Vote." In a public debate held in the Second Ward off South State Street, the two men openly competed for black votes, speaking words that must have seemed strange to new arrivals from the South.

One of the candidates decried the fact that no more than one hundred jobs were held by blacks in city hall. "What about the other 124,990 of you?" he asked the crowd. "We have come to the time when we no longer should recognize race, color or religions, but place every citizen on the same level so far as his constitutional rights go and his rights to have enjoyment of honest, efficient government. It is not a question of electing half a dozen Negroes to a political office, but the question of doing things for all of Chicago that will benefit the entire Negro population of this city. . . . It is a question of treating all people alike." That kind of public dialog must have seemed shocking to new arrivals like Dempsey and Lil.

Crime was one subject on which Chicago and Memphis did not noticeably differ. It had a high public profile because there was so much of it. The newspapers were filled with stories of violence, graft and corruption, police raids, and public lynchings.

In Collinsville, a southern Illinois suburb of St. Louis, a man was lynched in 1918 because he was feared to be an "enemy alien." It was a big story in Chicago, where there was a large immigrant population. The paranoia that surrounded World War I was so great that a Chicago merchant was arrested that same year and sent to jail for making "seditious remarks" about the conduct of the war.

Police raids against South Side bars were commonplace when Dempsey and Lil moved to the neighborhood. Usually the police looked the other way to minor violations, but when more serious crimes were involved they struck with major force. In the January 19, 1918, edition of *The Chicago Tribune* there is an account of a South Side raid that resulted in the seizure of twenty-eight slot machines at nine saloons and pool halls.

"At the saloon of Walter Hoijnack, the proprietor engaged in a fight with two deputies while a woman reached into the cash drawer for a revolver," reported the newspaper. "A constable drew his revolver in front of the saloon of John Clausen and threatened to shoot the first deputy who entered. They rushed at him and he fled."

Dempsey didn't have to frequent the saloons to know what was happening inside. All she had to do was read the newspapers.

Not yet appearing in the newspapers were the crimes taking place beneath the surface—the so-called organized crime associated with illegal whisky sales. In 1918, Chicago was neither "wet" nor "dry," but rather something in between, with permits issued by the city to bars that met local requirements for liquor sales. That came under attack by the federal government, primarily because of fears that the performance of the nation's fighting forces were being affected by liquor sales.

Chicago resisted ending its permit system, but it became a moot issue in January 1920 with the passage of the Volstead Act and the arrival of Prohibition. Prior to Prohibition, most of the illegal crime in Chicago centered around gambling and bootlegging meant to skirt existing taxes and regulations. Prohibition represented an economic boom to organized crime families around the country. Hundreds of millions of dollars were at stake.

Although organized crime operated in Chicago, New York, and Memphis with relative immunity prior to Prohibition, as a business enterprise it exploded as Americans ignored the ban on liquor and paid any price asked for bootleg products. Nowhere was the market more expansive—and the competition more entrenched—than in Chicago.

One of the most notorious underworld figures prior to Prohibition was Big Jim Colosimo, a restaurateur and racketeer who controlled a significant portion of South Side vice. When the competition turned violent in 1915 and Colosimo was blackmailed by rival gang leaders, he sent for Johnny Torrio, a young, New York mobster who had a reputation as a very effective street fighter.

Torrio solved Colosimo's problem by killing the blackmailers. Hailed as a hero by his boss, Torrio quickly rose through the ranks and established himself as a major player. One of the lieutenants he brought into the organization was another street tough from New York named Alphonse Capone.

Colosimo, with the help of Torrio and Capone, ruled the South Side with impunity. Although Colosimo was the undisputed boss of prostitution, gambling, and bootlegging in the city—and ran those operations from his café, named Colosimo's—he never truly felt comfortable in the role of a rackets' boss.

Colosimo's true passion was music. As the impresario for his own café, he not only auditioned and approved each musical act that performed in his café, he more or less acted as a musical god-father for the entire music scene. If you were a musician, Colosimo could open doors for you or he could shut them permanently.

One day he auditioned a singer by the name of Dale Winter, a pretty, big-bosomed twenty-five-year-old with huge ambitions. Colosimo not only hired her to work in the café, he fell in love with her and ditched his wife so that he could marry her. In many respects, Colosimo was a Gatsby-like character,[3] well known about Chicago but tainted by his past. His top priority became his relationship with Winter. She deserved to be a star, he felt, but he feared that his background would stand in her way.

When Prohibition shut down legal bars in Chicago, Torrio saw an opportunity for his boss to make a fortune, not just from manufacturing bootleg liquor but from stealing existing stocks from warehouses and from smuggling operations across the Canadian border, where alcohol was legal.

Colosimo balked at Torrio's pleas for expansion, stating that he already had plenty of money and wanted no more trouble from federal revenue agents. In truth, he was fearful of damaging Winter's career ambitions or, even worse, losing her. That wasn't the response Torrio wanted, so he arranged for his boss's murder. Colosimo was gunned down at the front of his café only one week after he returned from his honeymoon with his new bride.[4]

As the new boss, Torrio engineered a coalition of Chicago's ethnic gangs into one centrally controlled organization. Illegal alcohol sales, prostitution, gambling, all came under Torrio's control. To make it work smoothly, he adopted the Memphis style of operations: government officials were corrupted on a grand scale by the use of payoffs and special favors.

None of this was anything new to Dempsey, who well understood the Memphis system, as did ever other African American who lived in the city. There were two ways the cities differed, however.

The first had to do with cocaine. In Memphis the narcotic was a major ingredient in underworld operations. It surely existed in Chicago, but at nowhere near the same levels. That is probably because of Coca-Cola, the Southern-based soft drink company that utilized cocaine as a major ingredient. Large amounts of the drug were imported from Columbia to the bottling plant in Memphis and eventually found its way into the Beale Street economy.

The second way organized crime in the two cities differed was in the ethnic breakdown of the underworld organizations. Italians led the operations in Chicago—as they did in New York and New Orleans—with the assistance of satellite gangs composed of Jews and the Irish. The opposite was the case in Memphis, where the Irish and Jews ruled with little input from Italians.

When they arrived in Chicago, Lil was nineteen and still obsessed with music. She was an attractive woman who possessed a brightly expectant face with dancing eyes that always made her appear much younger. Because of her unabashed eagerness to learn, her precociousness, and her slender frame (at the time more corpulent women were in vogue), there was a Lolita-like quality to her appearance that stayed with her for years. To older men, Lil must have looked downright *dangerous*.

Soon after they moved to Chicago—possibly in the second summer—Lil left the house one day to buy some sheet music.

Jones Music Store at 3409½ South State Street was one of the most popular in the city, primarily because its proprietor, Mrs. Jennie Jones, also booked musicians and entertainers. Lil requested a particular piece of music and then asked the demonstrator, a man named Frank, if he would play it for her.

When the quality of his performance fell below her expectations, Lil asked if she could give it a try. Lil played the piece for Frank, and he was so impressed that he offered her a job working in the store as a demonstrator. At first, she was hesitant to say yes because she knew that her mother would be opposed to her taking the job.

Frank asked if she went to school. Lil, who was twenty or twenty-one at that point, realized that he thought she was much younger. So she lied and said that she did go to school. Frank suggested that she go home and talk to her mother and ask her if she could perhaps work at the store in the afternoons after school.

Lil went home, but she didn't mention the job offer to her mother. Instead, she just killed a little time. At three o'clock she returned to the store and told Frank that her mother had said it would be fine if she worked in the store after school.

Frank introduced Lil to Mrs. Jones, who admonished him for offering a job to such a young girl. He responded that it didn't matter how old she was because she was very good at the piano. Skeptical of that, Mrs. Jones pulled out several sheets of music and asked Lil to audition for her.

To hear Lil tell it, she tore up the piano that day, attacking the keyboard like a schoolgirl possessed. Why a twenty or twenty-one year old woman would want people to think she was only a teenager seems odd at first glance, especially since women that age usually want to appear older. But the explanation may be rooted in Lil's insecurities as a pianist and by the fact that her very domineering mother treated her as if she were a teenager.

Besides, she wasn't physically developed like the other women her age, and that may have prompted her to regress somewhat in her image of self. Since she was living with her mother and had no job, she may have *felt* like she was a teenager.

Mrs. Jones was pleased enough with Lil's audition to offer her the job on the spot. "Honey, if you want to work, I'll pay you three dollars a week."

Lil accepted and hurried home to tell her mother. As expected, Dempsey was most unhappy, especially with a low rate of pay she felt was exploitive. Lil told her not to worry about the salary; she only wanted the job so that she could learn the sheet music they sold in the store. Never one to stand between Lil and what she perceived to be a legitimate music education, Dempsey reluctantly agreed to let her keep the job.

Initially, Dempsey must have been disappointed with Chicago. Race relations were just as bad in many ways as they had been in Memphis. During the summer of 1919, the year Lil most likely auditioned at the music store, passions were so heated that the city was torn apart by a race riot. The national guard was called out to quell the rioters, and the image of troops with bayoneted rifles standing on South Side street corners must have frightened Dempsey.

Dempsey's relationship with Lil was as complicated as anything ever dreamed up by Tennessee Williams. That generation of African-American mothers was tough on its children. Slavery was not merely an abstract historical fact. For many of them, it was a living memory, if not from personal experience, then from the recollections of their own fathers and mothers.

Such mothers felt a strong obligation to instill in their sons and daughters an appreciation of their freedom. They didn't want their children to be equal to the children of their white employers: They wanted them to be better. Dempsey's relationship with Lil was further complicated by the fact that she was her only living child. Perhaps even more important was the fact that Dempsey was a dreamer. She had learned to read and write at a time when almost all of her contemporaries were illiterate. She had failed to make her own life rise to the expectations of a dreamer, but in Lil she saw a second chance.

There was something special about Lil, and Dempsey was determined to protect Lil from both herself and the evil world that she knew existed outside their home, even if, from time to time, that meant abusing her with the business end of a broomstick.

Lil didn't tell Mrs. Jones that her real reason for wanting to work in the store was to memorize all of their sheet music. By her second day of work, she had done precisely that and learned everything in their music catalog. The customers, who thought she was cute and talented for her supposed young age, gave her a nickname—"Lil' ole Girl."

It was while she was working in the music store that she met her first music celebrity. By the time he was in his late twenties, Jelly Roll Morton had made a name for himself as a legendary rag-time pianist. There are those who believe—Morton among them—that he is one of the inventors of jazz. Certainly, he was among the first to play it in New Orleans. A light-skinned black of Creole ancestry, he stood out in his surroundings because of his dapper good looks and his unique style of playing the piano. No one else of that era was quite like Jelly Roll.

Jelly Roll eventually moved to Chicago, but the exact date is questionable. When Lil first met him, it is unclear whether he was then living in Chicago or simply there to perform in one of the South Side's glitzy nightspots. It was customary for musicians to hang out in the music store in the early afternoons. They took turns performing and compared notes on good places to work.

On the day Lil met Jelly Roll, he was slow to step up to the piano. He stood near the door for a while, she later recalled, and then sat down to watch and listen. Lil did not know who he was and barely noticed him until he decided to take a seat at the piano. Once he began playing, Lil knew he was someone special.

"I don't know what he played—what pieces they were, but they were loud and the place was rockin' and the people were jumping up, keeping up with him, and I was jumping higher than anybody," she later recalled.[5]

People came into the store from off the street, but it was already packed with people. "Oh, boy, it was quite a session," she said. "He played four or five numbers, and I'm listening, all intently, you know. I'm not missing a note, baby. So he played and laughed. He was getting more kick out of me jumping up and laughing, see, than anything. And he was playing and smiling and looking at me."[6]

To Lil, watching Jelly Roll was as daunting as hearing him. "It was the volume he played with," she said. "He hit the piano—well, his left hand and his right hand were both loud—and his feet were stomping."

When Jelly Roll rose from the piano bench, he brushed his hands together, as if to tell his audience, "Take that!" Lil was impressed. "I said, 'Whew!' and then they said, 'Oh, Jelly!' That was when I found out what his name was—Jelly Roll Morton."

Someone in the store shouted out, "Oh, Jelly! Listen to the little girl play now."

Lil was stunned. "Oh, my goodness," she said. "I can't possibly play myself. I can't play behind him."

The crowd was insistent, so she sat down at the piano.

"Naturally, I couldn't play any jazz, so I played a little classical piece," she recalled. "He just smiled and eased on out the door. Funny thing about jazz musicians, you know. They don't want you to cut them with anything classical. They don't want you to play anything they can't follow. So he just walked quietly out the door."[7]

From that day on, Lil knew exactly what she wanted to do with her life. Before that, all she knew was that she wanted to do something with music. "I imitated him after that," she said. "Boy, I only weighed around eighty-five pounds, and from then on you could hear all eighty-five of 'em."[8]

At last, Lil had direction in her life. For the next year or so, she worked hard to find a place for herself in music. It was probably a difficult time in the Hardin household. Dempsey recoiled at any mention of jazz or nightclubs—and with good reason. While music was the creative force on the streets of Chicago in those days, it was not the power that had the biggest influence. The Chicago underworld, represented by John Torrio and Al Capone, had a lock on the music and nightclub scene through its control of gambling, prostitution, and bootleg alcohol.

Even so, depending on your perspective, the Chicago music scene exploded. Whether that happened despite the influence of the underworld or because of its influence is open to debate. At the core of that artistic explosion was the black community's need for both self-expression and economic betterment. It was not entirely an African-American phenomenon (some of the new arrivals were white), but for the most part it was the result of a black exodus from southern music centers such as Memphis and New Orleans. Certainly, gangland violence was nothing new to the arrivals from those two cities. They had lived with it for years.

There were two types of entertainment in Chicago in those days. For the white, straight world there were symphony and ensemble concerts, poetry and dramatic readings, and high-gloss ragtime music. Typical acts at the Palace in 1918 were Eddie Foy and the Younger Foys, Fritizi Scheff, and Sarah Bernhardt. In April

1918 John Philip Sousa conducted his music for "dime" concerts held in public schools.

Entertainment for the city's black residents never made the big advertisements in the *Tribune.* South Side clubs operated by word of mouth and by posters. Mostly, if you were black, you paid your money and you took your chances. The music was gritty, unpredictable—and typically spectacular!

One of the top underground nightclub performers in Chicago when Lil arrived was Alberta Hunter. Shortly after arriving in 1912, she got a job singing at Dago Frank's, a club that catered mostly to prostitutes and pimps. After two years there, the police shut down the club and she went to a slightly higher-class club named Hugh Hoskins's, where she remained until 1916. By 1918, she was working at the Elite No. 2, where her reputation spread to the point where established stars such as Al Jolson and Sophie Tucker regularly dropped by to enjoy her music.[9]

Hunter was a blues singer, but during the first three decades of the twentieth century, the distinction between blues and jazz was imperceptible. Typically, blues was played slowly, with rhythmic, evenly spaced harmonics that enhanced gut-wrenching vocals, while jazz typically was upbeat, harmonically explosive, and devoid of vocals. If Hunter sang a blues song that had a breakout instrumental, nightclub patrons would probably, with some justification, called it jazz.

For Jelly Roll Morton, Chicago's musical counterbalance to Hunter, jazz was a style of music, not a specific composition. "Any kind of music may be played in jazz, if one has the knowledge," he said. "No jazz piano player can ever really play jazz unless they try to get the imitation of a band."[10]

The light-skinned Morton didn't want to be thought of as a blues musician, which to his way of thinking was associated with rural black poverty and ignorance. Sophistication was what set jazz apart, he thought, and the urbane, verbally proficient Morton made that clear to anyone who would listen.

Unlike the other arrivals from Memphis and New Orleans, Morton didn't take a direct route. Only after spending time in Los Angeles, where he pimped for prostitutes and ran a gambling house, did he travel to Chicago—and that was only because a Chicago-based publishing company offered him a large sum of money for the rights to "Wolverine Blues," a song he made popular with the New Orleans Rhythm Kings.

Morton found steady work in the clubs, but he didn't get along well with Torrio's Irish, Italian, and Jewish associates, who often lost patience with him for putting on airs. Sometimes he got fired before he ever played the gig, simply because of his incessant talking and fastidious mannerisms. The mobsters who ran the clubs were tough guys. Morton was too much of a dandy to ever be just another one of the guys.

The one place where Morton's fastidiousness paid off was in the studio. He did not have a regular band with which he recorded. Whenever the opportunity rose to record, he simply rounded up the individual musicians he thought would be good for the session.

"At rehearsal [Morton] used to work on each and every number until it satisfied," recalled drummer Baby Dodds. "Everyone had to do just what Jelly wanted him to do. During rehearsal he would say, 'Now that's just the way I want it on the recording.' And he meant just that . . . but [he] wasn't a man to get angry. I never saw him upset and he didn't raise his voice at any time. He wasn't hard to please and after making a record he would let us know when he was pleased with it."[11]

The other musical heavyweights who emigrated to Chicago from New Orleans during this time were trumpet man Joe Oliver, better known as King Oliver, and cornet player Freddie Keppard,

known as King Keppard to his fans in New Orleans, where he performed with the popular Creole Orchestra. Keppard and Oliver
were relentless rivals in New Orleans, and when they both moved
to Chicago they continued the tradition.

By the time Joseph "King" Oliver left New Orleans he was a
rock-solid legend, the best trumpet player in town. He was a big
man who had a prodigious appetite: band members recall him
eating an entire chicken and apple pie at one sitting, then wash-
ing it down with eight or ten cups of coffee. He was the same
way about his music. He gobbled it up the way he did chickens
and pies.

As you can imagine, he was not very forgiving of band members who picked and nibbled their music. He was a tough taskmas-
ter, and he had a ferocious temper. Once band members ignored
his signal to end a song (it was a loud stomp). When he chastised
them, they said they were sorry but they simply didn't hear him.
Before the next gig, he arrived early and hid a brick on the bandstand. When the time came to end a song, he slipped the brick
from its hiding place and slammed it down against the wooden
planking of the bandstand. That especially unnerved the band
members because they knew he carried a pistol inside his jacket.
No one ever missed a signal again.

When King Oliver arrived in Chicago in 1918, he put together
a new band, King Oliver's Creole Jazz Band. (Creole was a popular word for use in band names of that era because, in addition to
maintaining as association with New Orleans, it diluted the racial
impact of being African American.) In fact, most of his band
members were from New Orleans—Baby Dodds on drums, his
brother Johnny Dodds on clarinet, Bill Johnson on bass, and
Honore Dutrey on trombone.

Thanks to the creativity of Alberta Hunter, King Oliver, and
Jelly Roll Morton, Chicago had a vibrant music scene. It was hardly

authentic "Chicago" music, but all that would change with time, especially when the city's white musicians got involved.

Louis Armstrong was born on August 4, 1901, in a rundown section of New Orleans that was as violent and inhospitable to new life as any place on the planet. His mother, Mayann, was only fifteen when he was born, and his father, William, abandoned the family early on, leaving Louis and his teenage mother to fend for themselves.

Those were terrible times for African Americans in New Orleans. Housing was crowded, and few structures were above the level of a shanty. Sanitation was unbelievably crude. Except for the positions of prostitute, cook, or cleaning woman, economic opportunities for women were almost nonexistent. Louis's father worked in a turpentine factory and had a regular income, but he never sent any money to Mayann.

Faced with that scenario, Mayann placed Louis with his grandmother, Josephine, and went off to make a living in the black section of Storyville—as a prostitute. New Orleans was a big city, but when it came to the gambling dens and whorehouses, it was a very small community indeed. No one can say for sure how long Mayann turned tricks, but the possibilities are good that she might have encountered Jelly Roll Morton in the performance of her duties.

Morton often played at the bordellos, as did most of the other musicians who, on a daily basis, were translating their life experiences into a music that we would later call jazz. Lil would be embarrassed in later years by Dempsey's seemingly parochial attitude toward jazz, but the truth of the matter is that Dempsey was correct to associate jazz with prostitution and gambling. Each was a part of the other.

The irony of it, of course, is that just as jazz eventually escaped that association to become a legitimate art form, gambling, in the form of casinos and lotteries, went on to become an accepted entertainment, as did prostitution when it later mutated into the adult entertainment industry with its domination of the multi-billion-dollar video and cable television market.

Within two years, Mayann had another child, a daughter she named Beatrice. Apparently, she kept Beatrice at her apartment in Storyville, for she was there when Louis left his grandmother's house around the age of seven to live with his mother. Growing up in Storyville was no picnic, but it was probably easier on children than it was on the adults, for whom shootings and knife fights were a daily occurrence. The only winners in his neighborhood were the pimps and gamblers. They made lots of money and didn't have to do any heavy lifting or dirty cleaning.

Louis was industrious his entire life. Upon his return, Mayann enrolled him in a boys' school and allowed him to work after classes. From the age of seven to eleven, Louis worked for a Russian Jewish immigrant named Morris Karnofsky. Louis helped him collect bottles and rags and rode with him when he delivered coal to the whorehouses.

The prostitutes made a lasting impression on Louis, not just because they were white but because they were so young. Most of the girls, he said, looked like they had just graduated from high school. Just laying eyes on them was a privilege, he thought, since it was a sight that was forbidden to other blacks. Traveling with Karnofsky opened doors to him that otherwise would not have been available.

Jews and blacks have a long history of animosity in the South. New Orleans was no exception. Even at that young age, Louis knew how blacks felt about Jews, but he liked the Karnofsky family and did not understand the reasons for the racial hostility.

"I had a long time admiration for the Jewish people," he wrote in later years. "Especially with their long time of courage, taking so much abuse for so long. I was only seven years old but I could easily see the ungodly treatment that the white folks were handing the poor Jewish family whom I worked for."[12]

One day Louis spotted something in a pawnshop that set his soul on fire. It was a battered old cornet, its brass blackened by time and neglect. For five dollars it could belong to Louis. When he told the Karnofskys, they advanced him two dollars on his salary, enough for him to purchase the instrument on the "lay-a-way" plan, whereby he paid two dollars down and fifty cents a week until it was paid in full.

The Karnofskys helped him polish the instrument and clean its valves, and they encouraged him to learn to play it. Sometimes they allowed him to sing Russian folk songs with them. It was rare at that time for a black child to bond so intimately with a white family, and it had an effect on Louis that influenced his perception of whites for the remainder of his life.

When Louis was eleven, the Karnofskys bought a home in the white section of town and Morris went into another line of work. That meant they no longer had a reason to provide Louis with a job. Without a job, Louis dropped out of school—he was only in the third grade—and took to the streets, joining the other child hustlers who did whatever it took to make a few pennies. The police in that district got to know him quite well. On one occasion, Louis was caught firing a pistol. For that, he spent a night in jail before being taken to court. Since he was a juvenile, the judge sentenced him to an indeterminate term in the Colored Waif's Home.

When he lay on his bed at night in the home, he sometimes heard Freddie Keppard blowing his horn at nearby lawn parties. He decided then that what he wanted to do more than anything else was be a musician. But when he asked the band director at

the home if he could join the band, he was told no, that his reputation was too bad.

Louis persisted. Finally, the band director relented and
allowed him to try the tambourine. He progressed from that to
several other instruments, eventually settling on the cornet. He
was so good that the director made him the leader of the band.

Accounts vary as to how long Louis was an inmate in the
Colored Waif's Home, but two years seems the most logical length
of time. After his release, he moved back into the home with his
mother and sister and did what he could to help support the family. Of course, there were not many opportunities for teenage
workers at that time, so he held down a variety of part-time jobs
such as delivering newspapers, unloading banana boats, and selling coal on the streets.

What he really wanted to do was make a living as a horn
player. There were various ways to do that. Marching bands regularly paraded up and down the street. Bands played for private
parties and picnics. They played for funerals and weddings. Often
they performed from mule-drawn wagons that were driven
through the streets in an effort to draw customers to a nightclub,
restaurant, or business conducting a sale it wanted to advertise.

Often when Louis performed, the Karnofskys showed up,
applauding along with everyone else. Before leaving, they always
asked if he needed anything. Early on, Louis figured out that white
people did not like all blacks, but did like some blacks. He always
thought it was in his best interests to be in the group they liked. He
had a similar attitude toward whites. He didn't like them all, but
some he did like. Throughout his life, he made it a point to have
whites in his support system, despite criticism from other blacks.

In some respects King Oliver felt the same way. Even when
he was at the top of his game in New Orleans, he worked as a
yardman and butler for white families. He was a big, tough man

who had a violent temper, but he never directed it toward whites. To Louis, he was a role model and a father figure—a black man who could move within the white community by virtue of his wits and musical talent, and within the black community by virtue of his brute strength and street smarts.

When Oliver spoke, Louis listened. Fortunately for Louis, Oliver took a liking to the youngster and allowed him to substitute for him when he was unable to play with Kid Ory's Band. Sometimes he took Louis home with him to eat with his family.

By the time Louis was sixteen and seventeen, he was performing on a regular basis, but mostly in the dives that couldn't afford the top bands. It was a tough way to make a living. Fights were frequent and often resulted in stabbings and shootings. At one point, Louis decided to supplement his income by pimping for a prostitute.

That didn't work too well because he was not very assertive and the prostitute was not very attractive. "She was short and nappy haired and she had buck teeth," said Louis. "Of course, I did not take her seriously, nor any other woman, for that matter. I have always been wrapped up in my music and no woman in the world can change that."[13]

When King Oliver left New Orleans and moved to Chicago in 1918, Louis replaced him in Kid Ory's Band. Louis was only seventeen, but he was quickly making a name for himself. Since playing with Kid Ory was not a seven-day-a-week gig, Louis also worked with other bands, performing in a variety of dives in and around New Orleans. It was at one of those dives, a whorehouse and gambling din named Brick House, that he met twenty-one-year-old prostitute Daisy Parker.

Their relationship began as a business transaction, with Louis retiring to her room for paid sex after each Saturday night performance. Daisy was a light-skinned black woman with a slender frame and attractive facial features. Although it became apparent to Louis early on that she had a violent temper and was jealous of other women he spoke to in the whorehouse, he just could not see beyond the passion he felt for her.

Unlike Louis, who could read and write, Daisy was illiterate. They were married in 1918, the same year Louis's mentor, King Oliver, abandoned New Orleans for the bright lights of Chicago.

After Jelly Roll Morton's visit to the music store, Lil knew she had done the right thing taking the three-dollar-a-week job demonstrating sheet music. Musicians came into the store on a regular basis, sometimes to buy music but other times to socialize and to play the upright piano, which, according to Lil, had no broken keys and was in pretty good shape. She not only met a lot of musicians in the store, adding to her growing knowledge of the musical hierarchy of the city, she got to hear different music styles.

With each passing week, Lil's self-confidence grew. Not only did she play the sheet music requested by the customers, she entertained them with her conversation and flattered them with her questions. Mrs. Jones quickly gave her a five-dollar raise, bumping her weekly salary to eight dollars.

Because of the way the store was designed, it was inevitable that Lil would become the store's star attraction. "[It] was a small place," she said. "They had music in the window and the piano and the player [sat] over at the side. As you came in the door, the piano player was over to the left near the window." That made Lil the first person a customer saw entering the store and the last person they spoke to upon leaving the store.

It is impossible to know how much of Lil's early success at the store was due to her musical abilities and how much was due to her personality, which could be alternately charming and ingratiating. She encouraged Mrs. Jones to get her a booking with a band, and she agreed to keep her eyes open for a good job for her.

During this time, Dempsey was under the impression that Lil was working at the store so that she could make enough money to return to Fisk University to pursue her education. She tolerated Lil's obsession with music because she thought it was a means to an end. If playing the piano in the store helped her return to school, then so be it.

If Lil was telling her mother during this time that she planned to return to school, then it is possible that she told Mrs. Jones the same thing. That may have been the reason Mrs. Jones agreed to help her find a booking with a band, so that Lil could make enough money to return to school.

Not every Chicago band had a piano player, though most probably wanted one. Of all the instruments that could be utilized in a jazz band, piano was the least available to would-be black musicians growing up in the ghettos of Chicago, New Orleans, or Memphis. Pianos were expensive, which made them a "white" instrument. And they were too large and bulky to be transported to nightclubs. The only place that black children had access to pianos was in church or in the homes of white employers.

There was a second difficulty with using pianos in jazz bands. It was perceived to be a woman's instrument. Not many black men at the turn of the century took piano lessons or played for their churches. The Jelly Roll Mortons of the world who adopted it as a male instrument did so by virtue of their ability to talk their way into business establishments, such as whorehouses, that had pianos available for female employees.

When Mrs. Jones began her search for a booking for Lil, the first obstacle she encountered was finding a band that wanted a piano player. The second obstacle was talking the band into hiring a *female* for the position. Women singers were commonplace in

Chicago, thanks in part to the success of Alberta Hunter, but female piano players in otherwise all-male bands were nonexistent. Whoever hired her would be taking a big chance and breaking all the rules to do so.

As providence would have it, Lawrence Duhe and his New Orleans Creole Jazz Band came into the store to audition for Mrs. Jones. They wanted her to book them into local venues. Lil happened to be there that day. She knew who they were, of course, for they were the first black, New Orleans jazz band to make it big in Chicago. She had never heard them perform, but she knew them by name: they were legends. From their humble beginnings as a marching band, they had risen to the status of a first-rate nightclub act. One thing that made them different was their willingness to incorporate a group of female singers into their act.

Lil was disappointed when she met them in the store. They were older than she expected, and they all seemed tired and in bad health. Lawrence Duhe she described as "skinny" and "always smiling." Sugar Johnnie Smith, the cornetist, was a "long, lanky dark man with deep little holes in his skinny face."[14] Rounding out the band were Roy Palmer on trombone, Tubby Hall on drums, Jimmy Palao on violin, and Ed Garland on bass. Of all the players, it was Smith who disturbed her the most, for there was something about him that was different. He was, in fact, a homosexual who was dying of tuberculosis at the time they auditioned in the store.

Mrs. Jones booked the band at a West Side Chinese restaurant. When their group of female singers joined them, they discovered that the clientele and the atmosphere of the restaurant were such that they needed a piano player, so they asked Mrs. Jones to send one over. She did, but he didn't work out because he was Chicago trained and didn't fit in with their New Orleans style of music. Neither did any of the other male piano players she sent. Finally, she gave Lil a break and sent her over to the restaurant.

That was what Lil had hoped and prayed for all along. "I learned everything [the store] had in two days because I didn't intend to keep the job very long, you know," she later admitted. "I just took the job so I could learn all the music."

Lil was not from New Orleans, so she did not play in that style. But her Memphis upbringing, which had exposed her to improvisational rhythms and instrumentation, had influenced her style of playing in ways she was not even fully aware of. Even if she never entered a Beale Street club, she heard the music on the streets. It was as much a part of the atmosphere of the city as was the unbearable heat and humidity.

Lil had something else going for her. Although she was undeniably attractive in appearance and feminine in behavior, often to an extreme, she was masculine in outlook and played the piano in a masculine, hard-driving way that was unheard of at that time. Even if she were dressed in frills, there was nothing frilly about her playing. Creatively, she was a hybrid—part man, part woman.

When Lil arrived at the restaurant, she was horrified to learn than none of the band members could read music. That was not unusual. Very few black blues and jazz players of that era could read music. Mostly, they just played from their gut.

Lil knew she was in trouble the moment she sat down at the piano.

"What number are you playing and what key is it in?" she asked.

"Key?" answered Duhe. "I don't know what key. When you hear two knocks just start playing."

Whether they actually didn't know the key or not—even musicians that do not read music typically know what key they are playing in—the band members had a baptism by fire planned for Lil, who played all over the keyboard, slipping in and out of every possible key in an effort to keep pace with the men.[15]

After the audition, Duhe asked her how old she was.

Lil never disclosed what age she gave, but her true age was twenty. Probably she said she was much younger since that is what she told Mrs. Jones at the music store. Even if she gave her actual age, twenty was still younger than the legal limit of twenty-one. She was underage anyway. What would be the harm in making her age sixteen or eighteen? Performing in the restaurant was no problem, but working at a nightclub such as the De Luxe Café would present problems.

"Oh, they will put us under the jail," one of the men said about working with Lil.

The law aside, the band's desperation for a piano player got the best of them and they offered Lil twenty-two-and-a-half dollars a week as their regular piano player. The band members agreed to keep her age a secret, but for them to pull that off, Lil would have to make certain that her mother did not find out about her new job; they had heard enough about Dempsey from Lil to know that she would be trouble.

That secret lasted three months.

One night a friend of Dempsey's spotted Lil playing with the band. When Dempsey questioned Lil about it, she told her mother that it was true, she was playing with the band. But, she lied, it was not what she thought—it was merely an exhibition.

Dempsey believed her.

The following week, a second friend told Dempsey the same thing. Lil was seen playing piano with a cabaret band. When Demspey confronted Lil with that information, Lil burst into tears. Dempsey asked her why she was crying. Lil told her it was because she knew she would make her quit.

Dempsey was outraged that Lil would squander the education she had provided her by working in a cabaret. She told her she would have to quit that very day.

Lil pleaded with her. Music was the most important thing in the world to her. Despite the money Dempsey had spent on her education, she really had no job skills other than music. Did Dempsey want her to become a cook or housekeeper like her?

It presented a real dilemma for Dempsey. Her reaction to Lil playing in a cabaret was based on her very strong Christian beliefs and what she had seen happen to innocent young girls who worked at the clubs in Memphis. Nightclubs and the people they attracted were evil, there was no question about that in her mind.

On the other hand, Lil had a point about her prospects for the future. Just as strong as Dempsey's beliefs about the evils of nightclubs was her commitment to Lil and her desire to see her daughter rise above the limitations of her own past. Was it even possible for the granddaughter of a slave to find the kind of success that Lil dreamed about?

In the end, Dempsey balanced her fears with Lil's dreams and agreed to a compromise. Lil could perform with the band at nightclubs such as the De Luxe Cafe, but only on one condition: Lil would have to allow Dempsey to pick her up at work each evening. Lil really had no choice but to agree.

From nine until shortly before one, she was the "Hot Miss Lil." When the clock struck one, she once again became Dempsey's baby girl. Like clockwork, Dempsey would be standing in the doorway when Lil got off work. Humiliated, Lil eventually persuaded her to wait downstairs. "I didn't want the people to know that she had to come after me after me being so hot all night."[16]

"Hot Miss Lil" Takes on Chicago

The leap from schoolgirl-turned-music demonstrator to piano player for the hottest jazz band in Chicago would have been a huge undertaking for anyone, but for a twenty-year-old woman who had basically never been out of the house—had never been inside a bar and hardly even dated—it was nothing short of miraculous. Lil or "Hot Miss Lil," as she had begun calling herself, was a sensation among nightclub patrons unaccustomed to seeing a gender-mixed band.

With her hard-pounding hands on the piano, youthful face, and slender body, she was an attraction all unto herself. She played like a man, but dressed like a Sunday school teacher. Dempsey's unrelenting diligence had paid off: almost overnight, Lil transformed into an articulate woman who dressed with modest sophistication and engendered an air of elegance. If she was at heart still a child who lived at home with her mother and ran away anytime a man looked at her too long, that would be her and Dempsey's secret. To the rest of the world, she was Hot Miss Lil.

Despite Lil's success as an entertainer, Dempsey continued to show up at the club each morning at one o'clock so that she could escort her daughter home. It was a remarkable relationship anyway you look at it. Dempsey was domineering, fearful of a world she felt was evil to the core, and yet she frequently compromised with Lil on issues that were important to her daughter. Lil, on the other hand, was strong-willed without being domineering, and she viewed the world as a kind place filled with opportunity. The two women were polar opposites, yet somehow managed to treat each other with respect.

Lil sometimes couldn't believe her good fortune. Although all the members of the New Orleans Creole Jazz Band were older men, respectful of tradition and disinclined to the excesses of youth, their music was loud, brash, and unrestrained. Lil, with her smiling face and animated gestures, was their biggest fan, and whenever they saw her getting so much into their music it usually pushed them up a notch or two.

"I had never heard a band like that," said Lil "They made goose pimples break out all over me."[1]

Frequently on the bill with the Creole Jazz Band at the De Luxe Café was piano great Tony Jackson. Once the band wrapped up its set, Jackson took the stage and played for a group of female singers. Lil remembers him playing songs such as "Pretty Baby" and "You Mean So Much To Me."

"All around I think Tony was a better pianist [than Jelly Roll Morton]," says Lil. "Jelly was a good composer, too, but they were just different. Tony was very talented, very talented. Their techniques were different. . . . Tony played a different kind of phrasing. He could play loud, or he could play soft. . . . Tony was, of course, not what you call a band piano player. I never heard of him playing in a band. He always played alone, you know. He was more of a soloist. He didn't have the strength of Jelly Roll."[2]

By this time, Jelly Roll Morton was as well known in Chicago as he had been in New Orleans, but his bookings had fallen off because of his inability to get along with the underworld bosses who owned the clubs. "Everybody talked about Jelly, all the musicians I worked with, but it seems that most of them knew him down in New Orleans when he used to play at the houses," says Lil. "When they'd start talking about piano players they'd always bring Jelly in."[3]

After a string of successful engagements at the De Luxe Café, the New Orleans Creole Jazz Band was booked at Dreamland, a larger, more upscale club located across the street from the De Luxe. When that happened, Lil really felt she had made the big time. She pleaded with her mother to stop coming to the club each night to take her home. None of the other band members had mothers waiting for them at the door. Besides, she was twenty-one now, old enough to legally do anything she pleased.

Dempsey, who was only forty-six, didn't buy that argument, but once again they compromised. Lil took the drummer, Tubby Hall, home to meet Dempsey, and he promised her he would personally escort Lil home after every performance. Hall was a mature, very pleasant gentleman, so Dempsey agreed. She would continue to wait up for Lil, but at least she would not be out on the streets.

By this time, the band was beginning to come apart. Sugar Johnnie died and was replaced on cornet by Mutt Carey and then Freddie Keppard. Tubby Hall left and was replaced by his brother, Minor Hall. That, of course, meant Lil lost her after-hours escort. Minor graciously agreed to see Lil home as his brother had done.

Unable to get along with either Carey or Keppard, Lawrence Duhe brought in a new cornet player, the renowned King Oliver. Lil had never met him before, but she certainly knew him by reputation. To her surprise, Oliver was quiet and non-confrontational. He just played his music and left without getting involved in the politics of the band. Then he underwent a personality change. He became critical of other band members and accused them of being undisciplined.

For some reason, Oliver did not like the trombone player, Ray Palmer. He needled and criticized him until Duhe felt he had to let him go. Lil's dream job suddenly became a nightmare. "I don't know what happened to make the band break up," she says. "But there were so many substitutes, one going this way, one going that way."

Finally, Duhe got so fed up with the strife that he quit his own band.

Oliver renamed the group King Oliver's Creole Jazz Band and booked it at two lesser-known clubs, the Royal Gardens and the Pekin, a late-night club favored by racketeers. At first, Lil stayed behind at the Dreamland Ballroom, working as a house pianist. Also performing in the club was Alberta Hunter. Like Lil, she had worked across the street at the De Luxe Café, but when Dreamland owner, Bill Bottoms, invited her to perform for him, she jumped at the chance.

"That's where the Lord put His arms around me," Alberta says. "Honey, I went from there to everything. I just sang and sang and sang."[4]

It was there that Lil and Hunter first met and shared stories about growing up in Memphis. For the most part, the Chicago music scene was made up of male musicians from New Orleans. By virtue of their birthplace and their gender, Lil and Hunter were in the minority. Lil was impressed with Hunter's vocal range and with her ability to make money (Lil once saw Hunter receive a three hundred dollar tip). Hunter was struck by Lil's beauty, though probably not in a way that Lil appreciated (at that point in her life Lil probably didn't even know what being a lesbian meant); and she was impressed by the way she played the piano.

"And she was a pianist, too, baby," she says. "You know one thing? All you had to do—we knew nothing about arrangements, keys, nothing—all you had to do was sing something like 'Make Me Love You,' and she would have one gone. She could play anything in this world and could play awhile. She was marvelous."

On stage, Lil and Hunter were a good match. If Hunter had a new song, she would walk over to the piano where Lil was seated and she would hum her a few bars of the song. Hunter was like all the other musicians: not only could she not read music, she was clueless about what key a particular song was in. It all came from her heart—and without benefit of a microphone.

For Lil, who played by ear as well as she read music, a couple of bars were usually enough. Hunter would sing, Lil would follow; then the entire band would join in. In those early days of jazz, singers and musicians often made it up as they went along. When Hunter was ready to end the song, she simply raised her hand. That was all that Lil and the band needed to wrap it up.

Looking back on Hunter's music, it is difficult to understand why so many people in both the white and the black community were so outraged by her songs. She was labeled a blues singer, but she never liked that label, since she sang many types of songs, only a few of which could be classified as blues.

It was probably the subject matter of her songs—sex, alienation, infidelity, and struggle—that garnered her the blues label. Of course, in those days a significant portion of the white population equated "blues" with "black." In the racial shorthand of the era, referring to someone as a "blues boy" or "blues girl," whether they were in the music industry or not, was simply another way of identifying them by the color of their skin.

Perhaps for that reason, blues singers, male or female, made a conscious effort to project images of smoothness, sweetness, and humility from the stage. Hunter was no exception. Writing for the *Pittsburgh Courier*, black journalist P. L. Prattis observed: "[Hunter] was friendly with everyone but indiscreet with no one. . . . every song she sang carried a message, and those to whom she sang took home the message and never forgot it. She paid for life's journey by comforting people and making them feel good all over."[5] Hunter made a similar observation about Ollie Powers, a male singer who worked at Dreamland with her. He had, she observed, "the most wonderful disposition you ever saw in your life and just as sweet as he could be."

The Dreamland was what would later be called a bottle club. Patrons could not buy alcohol inside the club; they had to take it with them in a paper bag. Unlike some of the other clubs, it catered to a racially mixed clientele. Frequently, white musicians from the uptown clubs visited Dreamland for the purpose of hearing the music and perhaps to pick up a few tips on this new music that was evolving from blues to jazz.

No one was turned away because of their skin color. Some people were turned away because of their profession. Not welcome were pimps and prostitutes, and go-betweens who found black women for white men. Club owner Billy Bottoms was a rarity in Chicago—a black man who operated an integrated nightclub. He worked hard to make his club a safe place for both entertainers and the people who came to hear them.

In a message to its readers, the Chicago *Defender*, the only black-owned newspaper in the city, had this to say about Dreamland: "Residents and business men of the Race throughout the city could feel safe in taking their close friends and the members of the family there with the knowledge that nothing would be allowed, by word or act, to cause complaint."

"There were almost never any fights," says Hunter. "People went there to have fun. Admittedly the fun got out of hand now and then when a person of one race passed to someone of the other, via one of the waiters or singers, a flirtatious note suggesting a rendezvous. The notes were called grenades for good reason."

One of the things that Lil admired about Hunter was her sense of style. She seemed determined to be one of the best-dressed women in the city. Once she paid eighteen hundred dollars for a coat made of mole and seal skins. Many of her gowns were tailor-made. "Alberta wore heavily beaded dresses that flittered and sparkled as she shimmied around the room and sang," Lil told jazz critic Chris Albertson. "Every now and then she'd make her breasts jump, and then the cats really loosened up on their bankrolls."

That was one thing that Lil and Hunter shared—an interest in money. Lil never hid the fact that money was the big attraction to playing in nightclubs. If she received personal satisfaction from the music she played, that was a bonus; but she never lost sight of the end goal. Lil was making one hundred dollars a week at that point, but Hunter was making much more. On a good night Hunter sometimes went home with four or five hundred dollars in twenty and fifty dollar bills.

On her days off from the Dreamland, Hunter often performed in other clubs around town. Usually, they were dives that attracted gangsters. She didn't mind what line of work her audience was in as long as they were good tippers. Often there were shootings and stabbing in the clubs where she worked.

One night the lights went out while she was singing. There was a loud bang, a pistol shot. When the lights came back on, a dead man was lying at Hunter's feet, and her hand was in the cigar box that contained the band's tips, money that was supposed to be divided equally among the singer and the musicians. She kept singing as they dragged him off, her hand still inside the cigar box. Hunter was no angel, as her band members discovered, but she certainly could sing like one.

Hunter often made trips to small satellite communities around Chicago; other times, when the booking paid decent money, she rode the train to other cities to perform. On one such trip to Cincinnati, Ohio, she fell in love with a waiter who had the "prettiest eyes" she had ever seen. One week later they were married. Hunter never slept with him, of course, and when she returned to Chicago, her husband came with her. They lived with Hunter's mother, though she never slept in the room with him, preferring her mother's bed instead. Eventually, he returned to Cincinnati, where he filed for divorce. Hunter was never really able to explain why she got married.

Also getting married while they were working together at Dreamland was Lil. Not much is known about her first choice for a mate, except that he was an aspiring singer named Jimmy Johnson. Apparently, they both lived in the household with Dempsey, who also got married some time prior to that to a man named Miller. By that time she was going by the name Dempsey Miller.

In 1921, Hunter went to New York to record for a black-owned record label named Black Swan. She never returned to Chicago, except to perform on occasion. The following year, she recorded for Paramount Records, which used her silky vocals to launch its series of "race" records.

Whether she realized at the time she was breaking new ground by becoming one of the first black women to record the blues is debatable since she was always more interested in the performance and financial aspects of her craft than in any intellectualized analysis of what she was doing. Not only did she make records herself, she wrote songs for other performers. For example, Bessie Smith's big hit, "Downhearted Blues," was composed by Hunter.

In 1923, Hunter replaced Bessie Smith in the Broadway musical *How Come?* A few years later, while visiting in London, she was offered a role in the London production of *Show Boat.* All the while, she continued to make recordings for Paramount.

By the end of the decade, she was an international star who was probably best known for her version of "Can't Help Lovin' Dat Man." Hunter retired from the stage in the early 1950s to care for her ailing mother. When her mother died in 1954, she gave up singing and enrolled in nursing school. For twenty years, she worked as a hospital nurse, not giving any thought to her music until the 1970s, when she made a comeback and wrote the musical score for Robert Altman's movie *Remember My Name.* She died in 1984.

Johnny Torrio's liquidation of Big Jim Colosimo barely caused a ripple in the Chicago underworld. With Prohibition now in place, there was enough money to go around for everyone. Torrio made certain that some of that money, in the form of payoffs (or campaign contributions as it later was called), was spread around where it would do the most good—with elected officials and cops.

By 1921, Torrio was operating as many as eight full-scale breweries, all under the protection of the Chicago police. Beer production was so efficient—and the demand was so high—that Torrio started up his own trucking company named World Motor Service Company. Cops sometimes were hired to ride shotgun on the trucks.

There were advantages to owning a legitimate trucking company. On those occasions when federal agents made arrests and seized the trucks, Torrio successfully argued that he had no idea that beer was being transported in his trucks. He said it wasn't his responsibility to screen everyone who leased a truck. Since the feds were never able to prove that Torrio had advance knowledge of the trucks' cargo, they were returned to him to be used again and again. Torrio knew how to make the system work for him. If the feds could not make the system work for them, that was their problem.

Al Capone was the man Torrio put in charge of his trucking company. One of his most important responsibilities was the purchase of new trucks. Individuals who paid out money in the name of the organization were deemed more important than those who collected it. By 1922, Capone was clearly Torrio's number two associate.

What Torrio and Capone were doing was clearly illegal, but they did not see it that way. Chicago residents voted in 1922 to amend the Eighteenth Amendment for the purpose of allowing beer and wine sales in their city. The referendum passed by a margin of five to one, but it carried no legal weight and could not be enforced. What it did do was allow Torrio and Capone to rationalize that they were performing an important community service. They were only giving Chicago what it wanted and needed, or so they said—and sometimes they may have believed that themselves.

Torrio may have been a hoodlum, but he was a brilliant businessman. He manufactured the product, transported it in his trucks, and sold it to nightclubs that were operating illegally, at least as far as the feds were concerned. Sometimes he owned the clubs outright; other times handpicked associates ran the clubs. That meant he was in control of production, transportation, and sales. What CEO in America would not have been envious of Torrio? The only remaining economic variable, competition, was controlled by the use of his own police force.

That's where Capone proved his worth to the organization, by knocking down the competition and making certain that the clubs that sold their alcoholic products were operated in a successful manner. Whatever the club operators wanted, Capone found it for them, whether it was prostitutes or some of the best music money could buy.

Capone was an ardent music lover, though his tastes ran more along the likes of operas such as *Rigoletto* and *Aida*.[6] Jazz refugees from New Orleans found him respectful of their race and easy to get along with as long as they showed up on time and played their best. Capone and his bodyguards frequently visited the clubs, where he sometimes spent the entire evening listening to music and tipping the performers.

An argument can be made that Capone was the primary sponsor of the growth of jazz in Chicago. Who knows what would have happened without him? He not only made certain that jazz musicians had steady income, he refused to stand in the way of efforts to racially integrate the clubs. Whatever kept the booze flowing was okay with him.

None of the musicians who emigrated to Chicago from Memphis or New Orleans were shocked by what they saw, for they had been around organized crime their entire lives. For them it was an economic issue, not a moral one. If the only whites who paid them to play their music and showed them some respect were gangsters, then whose fault was that? Often black musicians played for private parties for Capone. Fats Waller once anchored a three-day party for him. Capone paid him handsomely, and Waller respected him for that. Later, when he arrived in Chicago, Louis Armstrong had a similar high regard for Capone, whom he sometimes called that "cute little fat boy."

African Americans also liked him because of his "family values." It was widely known that he had brought his mother, four brothers, and little sister to Chicago to share his house with him. Later, when he married, he had a son named Albert that he was crazy about. They often were photographed together at public events, and anyone in the trenches of jazz who needed a favor only had to affectionately mention Albert's name, or Sonny as he was nicknamed.

There was another side to Capone, of course. He had a violent temper, even in the very early days, and he was not the type of person who suffered a perceived injustice. Early one morning in 1922, Capone was out carousing with friends when his car careened and crashed into a parked taxi. "Capone's companions wisely beat it," wrote Robert J. Schoenberg. "He rushed over to the cab, spoiling for trouble, his alcohol-sodden temper exploding. Revolver in one hand, the star (badge) of a special deputy sheriff in the other. Capone ranted at the taxi driver . . . still slumped over the wheel, so badly injured he needed a hospital. Capone threatened to shoot the man."

Luckily for the taxi driver, police arrived before Capone could shoot him. The driver was taken to a hospital, and Capone, then twenty-three, was hauled off to the police station, according to Schoenberg, where he was locked up, pending bail, to answer three charges the next day in court: assault with an automobile, driving under the influence, and carrying a concealed weapon. Capone was quickly bailed out of jail, and the case never went to trial. Any mention of the incident was expunged from the record.

It was not surprising that Capone resorted to threats of violence against the taxi driver. It was a way of life for both him and Torrio. In 1922, police identified thirty-seven murders in the city as gangland slayings. The following year, the total went up to fifty-seven. Throughout Prohibition, more than seven hundred deaths in Chicago were labeled as gang killings.[7] Not all of those slayings were done by Torrio's henchmen. Some were done by Torrio's rivals and were directed against his organization.

The more success Torrio achieved, the more he was targeted by his competitors, among them the gangs headed up by the

Irishman Dion O'Banion and the Gennas, James, Angelo, and Mike. It was with the Gennas that federal agents scored one of their first gangland successes.

That happened because two friends of Angelo Genna took a fifteen-year-old girl across the state line and "mistreated her," according to the girl who later went to the police. Shortly before the trial began, Angelo Genna stopped the girl on the street and threatened to kill both her and her family if she testified.

Not intimidated, the young girl went directly to the police. Angelo ended up serving a year at the federal prison at Leavenworth. When he returned to Chicago, he wore the federal "rap" like a badge of honor, demonstrating with bravado that the federal government's bark was much worse than its bite.

In truth, a gangster's worst enemy was other gangsters, not the police or federal agents. In 1923, the Irishman O'Banion set Torrio up for a raid at a brewery he owned. While he was out on bail, Torrio put out a contract on O'Banion. That hit resulted in open warfare between the two gangs, one that lasted until 1925, when Torrio and his wife were ambushed by shooters while returning home from shopping. Torrio was rushed to a hospital, where Capone stationed thirty armed men around him to keep guard.[8]

Torrio recovered from his wounds, but he was never the same after the assault. Only forty-three, he had amassed a fortune estimated to be in the thirty-million-dollar range. The warfare against both federal agents and rival gangs hardly seemed worth it anymore. He called Capone into his office and told him he was retiring. "It's all yours," he reportedly said. With that, Torrio packed up and moved back to New York, where he became a trusted financial advisor to Frank Costello, Charlie "Lucky" Luciano, and Meyer Lansky.

With that, Al "Scarface" Capone assumed command of the organization and proceeded to reshape it in his own image.

Not until after King Oliver reorganized the band did he send for Lil, who gave two weeks notice to Dreamland and then joined him at the Royal Gardens.[9] Except for Minor Hall on drums and Eddie Garland on bass, King Oliver's Creole Jazz Band was totally revamped. Oliver brought in Johnny Dodds from New Orleans to play clarinet, Davey Jones to play alto sax, and Honore Dutrey to play trombone. With the addition of Lil again on piano, Oliver had the hottest jazz band in Chicago, perhaps even in the entire country.

Why Oliver continued to keep the word "creole" in the band's name is a mystery—all of the band members were very dark-skinned, with the exception of Lil, who at times appeared very light-skinned in early photographs—but it may have been because many people associated the word with jazz.

Lil never talked much about being the only woman playing in a major jazz band, perhaps because she didn't want to draw attention to herself for anything but her musicianship, but it was a very big deal indeed. Women had been fronting blues and jazz bands for several years, but always as vocalists.

As an ensemble player, Lil was a pioneer. In later years, all-female bands came onto the scene with varying degrees of success, but it would be another seventy years before women found widespread acceptance as ensemble players in America—and, even then, it would occur in rock and country music, not jazz.

Why Lil? What was there about her that allowed her to break the gender bar? Most of the males she played with were instrumentalists who excelled as soloists. That was not Lil's major strength. For the most part, she stayed in the center one-third of the keyboard, always more interested in rhythm than virtuosity. That made her a driving force in the band.

Another asset was the fact that she had an almost perfect ear for music and could repeat anything that she heard. That did not make her unique, however. All the band members were expected to do that. What she added that was different was her ability to "see" music in musical notation. Being able to read music meant that she had a spatial grasp of what the band was attempting to do musically. Practically speaking, she was able to verbalize their music in terms of it having a beginning, a middle, and an end. She wasn't the soul of the band; she was the brains of the band.

There is no indication that Oliver ever had romantic feelings for Lil, but there is plenty of evidence that he was proud of the way her attractiveness added to the band's image, for he sometimes sent photographs of "Hot Miss Lil" to friends in New Orleans.

Lil always denied any romantic interest in the guys in the band, and considering her personality and her fastidious nature—and the ages of the men—that is just plausible enough to be true. Whatever the nature of her marriage to Jimmy Johnson (there is no evidence she ever adopted his last name), it did not seem to have a negative impact on her relationship with the other band members. When the gig was over, they went their separate ways. Says Lil: "I didn't see the fellows much after they left work, so I don't know too much about their personality at home or off the job."[10]

Sometime in 1920, probably toward the end of the year, King Oliver accepted a booking for the band in San Francisco. Lil was not too happy about leaving her mother and her husband, but she went nonetheless. It was the first time she had left home since enrolling at Fisk University. As it turned out, the first six months were disastrous.

Since they were interlopers onto the San Francisco music scene, the local musicians union did not want to accept them. Soon they started having problems with the band's name. They were performing at the California Theatre when a man in the audience started shouting at them. "I thought you said those guys were Creoles," he screamed out. "Those guys are no Creoles. Those are niggers!"[11]

Not knowing exactly how to respond, Oliver and Dutrey started speaking to each other in a language they hoped would pass for Creole, whatever that was. They had both heard French Cajun on the streets of New Orleans, so perhaps they offered their best imitation. Whatever it was, it worked, for the audience sat in silence and stared at them.

Episodes like that took their toll. Being called niggers was nothing new to them, but it was the sort of thing that happened only outside music venues in New Orleans and Chicago. Back home, when they were on stage, they were respected. No one would dare stand up and yell "nigger" at them back home, not in any club under the control of Capone and his associates.

Minor Hall was the first to pull out and head back to Chicago. To replace him, Oliver sent for Johnny Dodds' brother, Warren "Baby" Dodds, who had been playing the riverboats out of New Orleans. Johnny tried to talk Oliver out of hiring Baby by telling him he drank too much, but Davey Jones, who had performed with Baby on the riverboats, told Oliver that he was a first-rate drummer.

Oliver's call came at a good time, for Baby had just quit his riverboat job. His first performance with Oliver in San Francisco was at a "jitney" dance club, where couples paid to get onto the dance floor. Being the new man, Baby knew he had to deliver, so he began putting a little something extra into his drumming.

Soon dancers began leaving the dance floor to move closer to the bandstand, where they could watch Baby. "Some even asked who I was and where I cam from," says Baby.[12] "Quite naturally it made Joe Oliver feel very happy to see people leave the dance floor and stop to listen to me. Davey Jones said to Joe, 'I told you so.' My brother was dumbfounded. He later told me, 'How did you learn to drum like that?' I answered him, 'That was my inspiration: to show you someday that I could drum. And I did."

Baby left his wife behind when he joined the band, but he did so with the intention of sending for her once he got settled. He told her it would be about two weeks. Bookings for the band were so sporadic, however, that he never felt settled enough to send for her. When he wrote her to mail him some of his papers, she told him she had had enough; she informed him that their marriage of nine years was over.

Baby was not the only band member having problems. The San Francisco misadventure was taking a lot out of Lil, without giving her anything important to hang onto. She was having problems in her marriage and she missed her mother, the only person she ever really felt close to. It had taken a while for Chicago to feel like home, but after six months in San Francisco, she realized that Chicago was where she belonged.

Lil left King Oliver's Creole Jazz Band late in 1921 and returned to Chicago, where she got her old job back at Dreamland. Following her a few weeks later was trombonist Honore Dutrey. San Francisco was just more trouble than it was worth.

Whatever illusions Louis Armstrong had about marriage, they were certainly shattered quite soon after his union with Daisy. "I awakened one morning and Daisy had a big bread knife laying on my throat, with tears dropping from her eyes, saying, 'You black-son-of-a-bitch, I ought to cut your goddamn throat,'" says Louis. "That's why I always said the Lord was with me. Many times she and I went to jail from fighting in the streets, and my boss would have to come get me out."[13]

At eighteen, all that Louis knew about male-female relationships was what he saw and heard from the other men he was around—and that group consisted mostly of other musicians, pimps, and gamblers. Following their example, he beat Daisy every night and then made love to her so that they could get some sleep. It was a cycle that continued night after night and was responsible for Louis's many encounters with the police.

"I can proudly say though that I didn't steal—much," says Louis. "I didn't have to, and I was so busy trying to keep from getting hurt and blow my horn—those blues they liked then—until stealing never crossed my mind."[14]

New Orleans was changing rapidly and in ways that did not enhance the economic well-being of the city's musicians. Even before Prohibition resulted in the closing of "legal" clubs, the federal government had insisted, toward the end of World War I, upon a crackdown on whorehouses and gambling dens throughout the city.

The New Orleans night life continued unabated, of course, but it affected musicians because loud, jazzy music was not always what the owners of illegal clubs chose to offer to patrons. Sex and gambling did not attract nearly the attention on the street that a jazz band did. Even if a club owner had paid off the police in his precinct, he still had to worry about civic-minded passersby hearing the music from the street.

The "old" New Orleans that Louis and the other musicians had grown up with was changing. People said the city was changing "with the times," but that seemed to imply it was changing for the better and Louis and the other musicians didn't see it that way. If those changes were costing them money, how good could that be?

Louis did what most of the other musicians did: he took a job on one of the riverboats that made regular runs during the spring and summer months between New Orleans and St. Louis, and sometimes as far north as St. Paul, Minnesota.

Typically, the boats were lavish, three- and four-story paddle-wheelers with sleeping accommodations, dining halls, and ornately decorated ballrooms where bands performed and travelers danced. The boats made frequent stops along the route, always pulling into a small town or city at nightfall, thus exposing local residents to the music and gaiety they otherwise would find only in a large city like New Orleans.

Often the boats would take local residents aboard—for a price, of course—and cruise up and down the river for several hours in the evening. For that reason, their arrival was always a major event.

The first riverboat excursion that Louis joined was aboard the SS *Sidney*, where he played with Fate Marable's band. Also in the band were George "Pops" Foster on bass and Johnny and Baby Dodds (before they went to Chicago). Marable played piano and acted as bandleader, a position that kept him in almost perpetual opposition to the other players. Band members were expected to play the latest popular songs and waltzes, and if an individual player missed a note his paycheck was docked. If the player repeatedly hit sour notes, he was given the ax—quite literally, for he would find an ax in his chair on the bandstand.

None of that mattered to Louis, though, because Marable paid him fifty dollars a week, plus a five-dollar-a-week bonus if he stayed aboard for the entire trip, the largest paycheck of his young career. In addition, he received free room and board, as long as they slept on the boat. If they ever wanted to seek room and board off the boat during a stopover—and they often did—they had to pay for it themselves.

The excursions, which lasted from the fall of 1918 until September 1921, were good for Louis in a number of ways. First, it kept him away from Daisy for months at a time. If it bothered him that she continued to turn tricks while he was away, he never told anyone. Every day and night he spent away from her was another day and night away from certain self-destruction. Second, it exposed him to white society in ways that had been unavailable to him in New Orleans, where most of his experiences with whites had been with employers and benefactors, and with johns and tough club owners.

Aboard the SS *Sidney,* Louis and his fellow band members—and the roustabouts that did the manual labor aboard the ship—were the only African Americans. All of the guests aboard the ship were white, as were the evening guests who came aboard in the small towns. Louis had never been around so many white people in his life.

As long as they were in the South, making stopovers in Memphis and St. Louis, the racial climate remained much the same. It was when they headed north, through Davenport, Iowa, LaCrosse, Wisconsin, and Red Wing, Minnesota, race became an issue that seemed beyond their normal experiences. Many of those guests had never seen African Americans, much less black musicians.

"We had to listen to plenty of nasty remarks," says Louis. "We were used to kind of jive, and we would just keep on swinging as though nothing had happened. Before the evening was over they loved us. We couldn't turn for them singing our praises and begging us to hurry back."[15]

The only time they allowed African Americans aboard the boat was in St. Louis, where they had "colored excursions" every Monday night they were in port. That was always a special event for the band.

Aboard the boat, the band slept in segregated quarters with the black roustabouts and dined at a table set apart from the white employees. They were asked not to speak to white guests unless spoken to, and even then to respond with unqualified respect and deference. Those rules disappeared on "colored" night. All the dancers were black, and the band was allowed to interact with them and to have a good time. Says Baby Dodds: "It gave us an altogether different sensation because we were free to talk to people and the people could talk to us, and that's a great deal in playing music."[16]

It was during one of those Monday night performances that Baby developed what he called his "shimmy" beat. He had once seen a white man start shaking and shimmying on the dance floor because he did not know how to dance. Baby picked up on that and started shimmying while he played his drums, especially the bass, which he pounded with his left foot. When a crowd gathered around him that night, he knew he was onto something, even if it was only a novelty move designed to attract attention.

One evening, drum manufacturer Will Ludwig came aboard the ship, according to Baby, and asked the drummer if he could stomp his toe as well as his heel when he played. Baby told him he did not know why not.

Ludwig measured his foot on a piece of paper and showed him where he wanted to put another pedal. Later, Ludwig returned with a sock cymbal, or high hat as they subsequently were called. Baby tried it out, but didn't like it. When Ludwig asked him if he wanted to demonstrate it, he said no, convinced that if it proved to be a success—and it was a huge success—he would make no money from it.

Despite the best efforts of the band, it was inevitable that problems would arise. Sometimes they were racial. Other times they resulted from being in close confinement for weeks on end. Louis coped by turning inward and focusing on his music. Each week his playing became bolder and more adventuresome.

Of course, that was not what bandleader Marable had in mind. He knew that the guests who came aboard the boat wanted to hear familiar music, and they wanted to hear it played the way they always heard it. Musical experimentation was not good for business, and Marable was firm with the band when it came to how they performed.

Baby coped by drowning his frustrations in whiskey. With time, it became a serious problem. One night they pulled into an Iowa river town and Baby reported to the bandstand staggering drunk. He wouldn't listen to Marable, and when Louis tried to intervene he threatened to punch him out. Finally, the owner of the boat, Captain John Streckfus, came down to the ballroom and asked Baby to quit making a scene.

In front of all the guests, Baby cursed the captain, telling him what he could do to himself. With that, Streckfus, a large, muscular man, grabbed Baby by the neck with both hands and choked him until he collapsed and fell to the floor. Says Louis: "It was a gruesome sight, but nobody said, 'Don't choke him anymore.'"[17]

No one got fired after that incident, but it did seem to change the mood of both Streckfus and the band members. Once trouble like that starts, it's like any other type of job: it's just a matter of time before it falls apart.

Baby saw Louis undergo a lot of changes during the two years they were on the boat. Louis began interacting with the audience, shouting out words like "cat" and "jive" and "scat," words Baby had never before heard. He'd use them in phrases like "Come on, Pops," and "Come on, you cats." If Baby is to be believed, Louis's voice changed during one of their excursions after he took a patent medicine to cure a cold. After he took the medicine, says Baby, he had the gravel voice that stuck with him the rest of his life.

One thing his two years on the river did not change was his atrocious taste in clothes. He wore shabby jackets and worn collars when they were performing, when all the other men had sharp white shirts and new jackets. Everyone talked to him about his clothes, telling him it was an embarrassment; but he paid no attention to them and continued to wear the same dowdy clothes.

In later years, Louis never had much to say about why he left the boat after two years, but Baby said it was because Streckfus started telling them how to play their musical instruments. Mostly, it had to do with business. When Streckfus realized that some of the older passengers were not dancing the way the younger ones did, he asked them to play songs that had four beats to the measure. He thought it would enable the older guests to bounce with the music instead of trying to keep time to it with their feet.

Baby didn't much care for the suggestion, partly because he didn't think it would work and partly because he thought he and Louis were the stars of the band and it didn't seem right for a white man to be telling them *how* to play their music.

Biographers have differed on whether Louis and Baby quit the boat or were dismissed, but in the grand scheme of things it hardly matters. What is important is that when the SS *Sidney* pulled into New Orleans in the fall of 1921, Louis and Baby left the boat and never returned, thus setting in motion a chain of events that would revolutionize American music history.

When Louis went home to Daisy, he discovered that she had given up prostitution and moved out of their apartment. She now lived in the servants' quarters of her white employer. Before Louis could reach her new apartment, he was stopped on the road by a security guard who wanted to know what he was doing in a white neighborhood.

Louis told him the truth, that he was there to visit his wife, and the guard allowed him to proceed. To his surprise, he discovered that Daisy had adopted a teenage girl and was caring for her as if she were her own child. That wasn't an unusual thing in the black community. Several years earlier, Louis had adopted his niece's son, Clarence, a child that had been fathered by a white pedophile who had lured Louis's young niece into his home for sex.

Not long after his return he discovered that Daisy had taken up with another man, a cornet player who worked the same district with Louis. Louis did not mind the men she had sex with when she was a prostitute because they were paying for it and it was money into his own pocket. But this cornet player, who was not paying for it, was another matter.

Louis separated from Daisy and moved in with a woman named Irene. For the next ten months, he played at various clubs in New Orleans, including Tom Anderson's, one of the more popular gathering places for whites. Despite the glitter of its furnishing and the top quality of its jazz, it was a regular meeting place for the city's gangster elite.

Louis never thought much past his next gig, but occasionally offers came along that gave him pause. One night New York bandleader Fletcher Henderson passed through town and heard Louis at one of the small clubs. He offered Louis a job with his orchestra, but he turned it down because Henderson would not also hire a drummer he liked to work with. The drummer was just an excuse, for Louis did not want to leave town with strangers. He could appear outgoing and brash on stage, especially when he started tossing his scat talk at the audience, but he was essentially a very shy man who did not have much confidence in his ability to make it on the outside without a friend and ally.

Louis fell into a groove and it looked like he was destined to remain in New Orleans for the remainder of his life. Then one day in August 1922 he returned from playing in a funeral procession to find a telegram from his old friend and mentor, King Oliver. "Papa Joe," as he called him, wanted Louis to come to Chicago and join his band.

Louis had exchanged letters with Oliver ever since his relocation in Chicago. Most recently he had received a letter with a photograph of Lil enclosed. Oliver wanted to show her off to his protégé. Oliver had often mentioned the possibility of Louis joining them in Chicago, but he had never asked him outright. Now he was asking.

The offer scared Louis to death, but if there was anyone who could persuade Louis to leave New Orleans it was King Oliver. "I made up my mind just that quick," says Louis. "Nothing could change it. Joe my idol had sent for me—wow."[18]

While he was saying his farewells, the bouncer at a club named Matranga, shook his hand and offered him some advice: "When you go up north, . . . be sure and get yourself a white man that will put his hand on your shoulder and say, 'This is my nigger.'" Crude advice, but words that Louis lived by for the remainder of his life.

For his train ride to Chicago, he wore his best clothes—a brown suit, a straw hat, and tan shoes. He carried two suitcases: in one was his cornet and in the other were all his earthly possessions. His mother made him a fish sandwich to eat on the overnight trip (blacks were not allowed to enter the dining car). It was his first trip anywhere alone.

It's hard to know exactly what was going through his mind, what gave him the emotional strength he needed to make the journey, but when you consider that his marriage had fallen apart, as had the New Orleans music scene, with everyone who was half decent heading north, it is apparent that he really did not have many options if he remained in New Orleans. Did he want to play and march in funeral processions for the rest of his life?

When Louis stepped off the train in Chicago, he expected Oliver to be waiting for him. He was nowhere to be seen and for a moment Louis panicked. "I was just fixing to go back home— standing there in my box-back suit, padded shoulders, wide-legged pants—when a redcap Joe left word with came up to me."[19]

The redcap put Louis in a taxi and told the driver to take him to the Gardens Café on the south side of town. As they went through the streets Louis was astonished at the size of the buildings. He thought that buildings that large were surely universities. When the taxi pulled up outside the Gardens, Louis felt intimidated by the club's elegant facade. Then he heard the music and was shocked at how good it was.

Once inside the club, he didn't approach the band right away. He stood in the shadows, watching and listening. He felt out of place. All the band members were dressed in expensive suits and he could see the flash of diamond rings on the bandstand.

After the set ended, Louis approached the bandstand and was relieved to see that they all were happy to see him. Besides Oliver there was Baby Dodds on drums, Johnny Dodds on clarinet, Honore Dutrey on trombone, Bill Johnson on bass, and Johnny St. Cyr on banjo. Not there that night was Lil Hardin, who was still working at Dreamland. When the band started back up again, Louis was invited to perform with them. "I was so happy I did not know what to do," says Louis. "I had hit the big time."

After the show that night Oliver took Louis to a boarding house run by a Creole woman from New Orleans named Filo. She was as happy to see him as he was to see her and they talked for hours about New Orleans. It had been a long time since she lived there, but she wanted to know all the news. Before going to bed, Louis soaked for a long time in the boarding house's private bathtub.

Louis slept late into the afternoon. When he awakened, Filo greeted him with a hot ham sandwich covered with pineapple and brown sugar. Said Filo, who was determined to send him off on a full stomach for his opening night at the Gardens: "You got to do a lot of blowing and you need something to hold you up." [20]

Louis wore a tuxedo that night, an old, tattered garment he called a "roast beef." It was patched here and there, but he was convinced that no one in the club would get close enough to see how old and raggedy it really was.

At eight o'clock that night a taxi pulled up at Filo's boarding house to take Louis to the Gardens. Filo was as excited as he was. He had made the big time.

"Little" Louis Wins Lil's Heart

F irst impressions are not everything.

When Lil first met Louis, she thought he was a bumpkin. "I wasn't impressed at all," says Lil. Louis weighed two hundred and twenty-six pounds and Lil could not figure out why everyone called him "Little Louis." "I was very disappointed—I didn't like anything about him. I didn't like the way he was dressed. I didn't like the way he talked. I just didn't like him. I was very disgusted."[1]

Louis, on the other hand, was smitten by the sight of Lil. It happened before he ever met her. Earlier in the year, when Oliver sent him a photograph of Lil, he responded by asking Oliver to tell Lil that he liked her.

Oliver probably did not pass that message along to Lil, for she was still married to singer Jimmy Johnson. But he must have had a love match in mind when he took Louis over to Dreamland to meet her. Ostensibly, the reason for the visit was to ask Lil to return to his band for their engagements at the Gardens.

In person, Lil exceeded all expectations. Louis fell in love with her on the spot. She was everything he was not—slender, attractive, educated, and confident. The fact that he met her for the first time in Dreamland, the most famous nightclub in the world, to Louis's way of thinking, only added to her already considerable charms.

When Louis and Oliver left Dreamland, Louis's head was spinning. He had no way of knowing that Lil thought he was a hick from the swamp, and even if he did know, he probably would not have blamed her, for no one had a lower opinion of Louis than Louis himself. He knew what he felt, and that was all that mattered.

Several days later, Lil joined Oliver and Louis at the Gardens. She already had dismissed him as a potential love interest, and his abilities on cornet did nothing to alter that opinion. Besides, at that point in her life, Lil was more interested in the financial aspects of music than in any artistic notions to which it laid claim.

Louis paid close attention, but he had mixed feelings. He had heard that Lil's marriage to Jimmy was on the rocks, so in theory she was available, but he could only think about her so long without thinking about himself and that always led to trouble. All the other musicians were so much more sophisticated than he was. Who was he to be thinking about Lil? He was still married to a crazy, knife-toting former prostitute.

"Who was I to think that a big, high-powered chick like Lillian Hardin, who came to Chicago from Memphis, Tennessee . . . right out of Fisk University, valedictorian of her classes, who me?" says Louis. "I thought to myself. I just couldn't conceive the idea. That's all."[2]

One of the reasons that Lil did not immediately notice Louis musically was because Oliver used him in a secondary role, playing second cornet behind his lead cornet. They developed a system whereby Oliver would lean over to Louis when he was ready to play a solo, and Louis would improvise a harmony part to go along with it.

Exactly how Oliver would use Louis in the band had been a subject for debate among the other members. They knew that Louis was a better horn man than Oliver, but they weren't going to tell him that. Finally, they asked Oliver point blank: "What are you going to do with Louis?"

"It's my band," Oliver responded. "What am I going to do, play second?"[3]

Oliver had changed since moving to Chicago—he had developed a smoother music style and certainly his dress and mannerisms were greatly improved—but he was still detail oriented. He knew exactly what he wanted, and he expected the band to carry out his wishes without question.

Most bandleaders were just that—leaders of the band. What set Oliver apart was his concept of what a band should sound like, look like, and act like. He expected everyone to be well dressed and to be well behaved on the bandstand. The band itself was organized in a certain way on the bandstand to optimize sound quality and appearance: from left to right was the bass, Lil on piano, the clarinet, Louis on second cornet, Oliver on first trumpet, the trombone, and then the drums. The banjo was positioned just off the piano as close to the treble keys as the player could get. The band had a large repertoire and could play a four-hour set without ever repeating a song, unless, of course, they were asked to give an encore.

As smooth as Oliver seemed, there was still a brick-tossing side that the players knew existed beneath that slick veneer. One thing that had not changed since Louis knew Oliver in New Orleans was his penchant for keeping a loaded pistol in his instrument case. Everyone knew he had it, but they were never certain why until the day that Baby, John, Dutrey, and Louis got into a spitball fight on the bandstand.

"Some of the spitballs passed Joe so close that he could hear the whiz as they went by," recalls Baby. "Joe said, 'If some of you guys hit me in my good eye, I'm going to shoot you.'"

The band members laughed and said they did not believe him. Oliver opened up his cornet case and showed them the gun. That quieted things down in a hurry. The band members figured he really carried the gun to protect himself because of the large sums of cash he carried with him, but no one was certain enough of that to test his patience.

Lil looked at the band with more amusement than anything else. After work they went their separate ways. She knew little about their private lives and she was not especially interested in knowing what they did when they were not on the bandstand.[4]

Lil soon learned of Louis's interest in her, but she was having problems in her marriage and Louis just didn't fit into that picture at all. Besides, for the past four years she had been performing exclusively with male musicians, none of whom she found interesting enough to go out with romance in mind.

As for Louis's playing, she just did not get what the fuss was all about. "I probably would have never paid any attention to Louis's playing if King Oliver hadn't said to me one day that Louis could play better than he could," says Lil.[5]

Playing second to Oliver did not bother Louis in the least. He was making fifty-five dollars a week, more money than he ever made in New Orleans—Lil was being paid almost twice that, but he did not know it at the time—and he was playing the music that he loved and he was doing it with arguably the best jazz band in the world. Why would he take issue with playing second to Oliver, who, after all, was his hero? Besides that, he was having the time of his life.

When he returned to the boarding house after that first night with Lil and the entire band, Filo had a meal all prepared for him, complete with home brewed beer (made from malt, yeast, sugar, corn, and water). Louis enjoyed the meal, but Filo was too drunk to serve it and soon passed out on her bed.

The next morning, when she had sobered up, she told Louis that ex-prize fighter Jack Johnson lived up the street in a mansion. Louis was impressed. For a man who was used to struggling for every penny in New Orleans and fighting with his ex-prostitute wife, Chicago, with its friendly people and abundant wealth, seemed like the Promised Land.

Not long after moving to Chicago, Louis purchased a typewriter and learned to use it so that he could communicate with the people back home. He discovered he loved to write, and he viewed his letter writing as something of a hobby. In later years, he carried a concealed tape recorder in his pocket for the purpose of keeping track of his conversations and thoughts.

His earliest surviving letter is one he wrote in September 1922, only a few weeks after arriving in Chicago, to Isidore Barbarin, a respected member of the New Orleans jazz community. In the letter, he thanked Barbarin for answering a previous letter he had written, one Louis thought Barbarin had been slow to answer. Louis told him that he understood: "When a fellow is playing with a red hot brass band and they have all the work he don't have time to be bothered with writing no letters."

That wasn't the case with Louis. He also was playing in a "red hot" band, but he found plenty of time to keep friends in New Orleans apprised of his progress.

If King Oliver's comments about Louis's musical ability piqued Lil's interest, it was nothing compared with what she witnessed from the bandstand. Louis was clearly attracting the attention of the audience. Hot Miss Lil was no longer the main attraction.

Night after night, white musicians gathered in the nightclub to listen to the band. Lil couldn't figure it out. She watched them to see if she could determine what they were interested in, but frankly she did not have a clue.

Clarinetist Buster Bailey certainly knew. "Louis upset Chicago," he says. "All the musicians from Isham Jones's big band, for example, came to the Gardens to hear the band Joe had, and especially to hear Louis. . . . King Oliver and Louis were the greatest two trumpeters I ever heard together."[6]

Jazz bands operate on the principle that all the members follow the same path, but not necessarily at the same time. The music is a complicated weave of sounds, all different, but each dependent on the other. Musically, the Creole Jazz band was rock solid, even without Louis. What he added was the element of surprise.

Veteran musicians were amazed at the way he could follow Oliver's solo parts, improvising harmony and counterpoint around Oliver's notes. Louis had a unique talent for being able to play all around the notes. Sometimes the two men improvised at the same time. It was the musical equivalent of carrying a tray of drinks while running atop a speeding train. Somehow they always made it safely through to the end of the song

Without a doubt, part of the band's appeal also was due to its flamboyant stage presence. Oliver used lots of gimmicks to alter his sound—cups, hats, even bottles were used to make his cornet sound like various animals—and the band members were unusually animated while they performed, swinging, swaying, playing off each other for effect. Lil did not play off the other musicians; she played off the piano, arms pumping, feet tapping, looking as if she were doing something—maybe *it!*—with her instrument.

Louis was not singing yet, but his jubilant, always smiling face communicated with the audience in ways that words could never have done. Other musicians came to hear the Creole Jazz Band, for certain, but they also came to *see* it perform, especially the two most visually active members, Louis and Lil.

One night Freddie Keppard showed up at the Gardens without his instrument. He stood right next to the bandstand, his stiff posture reflecting his antagonistic mood toward Louis and his playing. After listening for a while, he approached Louis during a break.

"Let me have your trumpet," Keppard said.

It was an awkward moment. Asking for another man's horn is a little like asking for his girlfriend or wife—it is a musical faux pas of the biggest order. Louis didn't know what to do. He was new in town and didn't want to make enemies. He looked at Lil for guidance and she nodded yes, go ahead and do it. Louis handed over his trumpet.

"Freddie blew and he blew and he blew and he handed the trumpet back to Louis," says Lil. "I said [to Louis], 'Now go get him!' Never in my life have I ever heard such trumpet playing."[7] While Louis played, Freddie slipped out the door and never again asked to use Louis's trumpet.

The romance between Lil and Louis was slow to develop, primarily because Lil was not initially attracted to him. Part of it had to do with his five-feet-four, two hundred-plus-pound frame, but also factored in was her perception that he was a little too backward socially to be a good match for the "Hot Miss Lil." He was a country boy even though he had grown up in a city, and she was a city girl, at least to her way of thinking.

All that changed as she got to know him. She followed that beautiful music he was making all the way into his soul, and it was what she saw inside Louis that made her fall in love with him. It's not clear who initiated the first date (soon after Louis started with the band Lil separated from Jimmy), but it may have been

Lil since those first dates were for early morning breakfasts and dinners at the Dreamland Café, where Louis tipped the singers one dollar to sing for them.

You would not think that "Hot Miss Lil" would be a old-fashioned girl, but from the way she and Louis entered their courtship, it is clear that she was. No one has ever suggested that Lil was promiscuous at any point in her life, with all the evidence pointing to her being very selective in her choice of sexual partners.

Lil and Louis tried to keep their budding relationship a secret from the other band members, but they fooled no one. At first, the band members were cool to the idea of the two of them dating, and they reflected that in the icy way they reacted to them. But as time went by the relationship became more a matter of astonishment to them, primarily because they knew that Lil and Louis were so different from each other. They started kidding Louis about the fact that he was able to get to Lil and they were not.

"Lil and I was really in there by that time," says Louis. "She used to tell me her troubles concerning her married life, and I would tell her mine. It seemed as though we felt so sorry for each other we decided out of a clear skies [sic] to get together for good."[8]

The precipitating event for them moving in with each other was the unexpected arrival of Louis's mother, Mayann. Visitors to Chicago had returned to New Orleans and told Mayann that they had seen Louis in Chicago and he looked like he was really hungry. They said he looked "so bad." That so alarmed Mayann that she took the next train to Chicago. At the train station she flagged down a taxi and went directly to the Gardens. When she saw Louis on the bandstand, she dashed across the dance floor, a suitcase in each hand.

Both Louis and Oliver saw her coming at the same time, prompting Oliver to comment, "Oh, here comes the hen."

"I couldn't hardly believe my eyes," says Louis.

Mayann pointed at her son and hopped up on the bandstand to hug him.

"My God, son!" she exclaimed. "They told me you were dying. So I rushed here to see about you. But thank God you're really alive and healthy. Thank God!"[9]

Ever since his arrival in Chicago, Louis had received a lot of good-natured ribbing from Oliver, who was fond of telling Louis that he was his true father. With his mother on the stage, Louis saw an opportunity to give Oliver a taste of his own medicine.

Leaning over to Oliver's ear, whispering so that no one else could see, Louis said, "Well, Papa Joe, Mother's here. Shall I tell her what you've been saying?"

According to Louis, Oliver blushed "all over the place."

Once she saw that Louis was all right, Mayann decided to return to New Orleans the next day, but Lil and Louis talked her out of it. "Lil and I were close sweethearts by this time and were really in there with each other, " says Louis.[10] Together, they decided it would be nice if Mayann stayed in Chicago, at least for a while.

Louis put Mayann up in a hotel, and the next day he and Lil went apartment hunting. They found a nice apartment located at Forty-Third and St. Lawrence, and she and Louis filled it with nice furniture. Of course, it was Lil who did all the decorating. Louis professed that he had absolutely no expertise in that area. "Lil, being up north for such a long time . . . she was really up on things, the modern things, and she had such wonderful taste," says Louis.[11]

They decided not tell Mayann about the apartment until they had it completely furnished. Once they had picked out all the furniture, they had it delivered on the same day. Working together, they decided where each piece of furniture would go, scattering it about the three-room apartment in a configuration that suited Lil.

The last room they organized was the bedroom. Once they got the bed in place, they stood there for the longest time, staring at it. Lil was on one side of the bed and Louis was on the other.

Suddenly, they looked at each other, each knowing what the other was thinking. "Before we knew it," says Louis, "we were making violent, but beautiful love. . . . She was so beautiful to me at such a precious moment, one I'll never forget as long as I'm colored."

With their relationship properly consummated on Mayann's new bed (at least they had not yet put the new sheets on it), they decided to show it to her. Mayann had no idea what was going on, so when they took her by to see her new apartment, she was totally surprised. With tears rolling down her cheeks, she thanked Louis and her "future daughter-in-law." Said Mayann: "I never thought I would live to see the day that I would be the proud owner of such a fine lovely apartment like this, after living in those dilapidated houses down in New Orleans."

There was something about that shared experience of taking care of Mayann, and having their first sexual experience on her bed, that removed any existing barriers between Lil and Louis. After that, they knew they were a couple—and so did everyone else. For Lil, it might have been as simple as seeing Louis respond so thoughtfully to his mother. Whatever it was, Lil was in love, most likely for the first time in her life.

In 1922, when their romance began, Lil was twenty-four and Louis was twenty-one. They attacked their relationship with all the gusto of unbridled youth. By virtue of the fact that Lil and Louis both performed in the top jazz band in the country, they quickly achieved celebrity as the first "power" couple in jazz history.

You never saw one without the other. Lil and Louis played hard every night in the clubs, and every day, during their waking hours, they played just as hard as friends and lovers. They explored

Chicago, they explored each other, and they explored their music, all with great passion.

For Louis, whose only intimate experiences with women had been with prostitutes, it opened a whole new vibrant world. For Lil, who had never found a man that complimented her and made her want to love as much as she wanted to be loved, it was magical. They became inseparable and refused to go anywhere without the other.

One of the activities they enjoyed the most was going on picnics, especially those sponsored by churches or civic organizations. The picnics were more than simple gatherings at which couples and families sat on quilts and enjoyed basket lunches. They were events that drew all the "big wigs" in the black community.

Couples got all dressed up and paraded up and down the lawn, showing off their new clothes or new spouses. If the men were not drunk when they arrived—and most were—they soon had their fill of libations. Sometimes the picnics ended in brawls, as friends, buoyed by alcohol, resorted to fisticuffs when their debating skills waned.

At the conclusion of the picnic, the men loaded up their wives and girlfriends and raced each other off the picnic grounds, creating a dangerous situation for all the bystanders. The fights and racing always frightened Lil, but they usually had a good laugh about it when they returned home.

One of the biggest events they attended that year was an all-black automobile race held at the Harthorne Tracks. They had never seen an all-black automobile race (Louis had never seen a race, period), so they were not sure what to expect. Since neither of them owned a car, they took a taxi to the event.

When the race began, they were both thrilled to be there surrounded by thousands of racing fans. The excitement of the crowd, the roar of the engines, all melded into a potent stimulant. Louis had a half-pint bottle in his back bottle, but he hardly thought about it because of the activity in the stands and on the track.

The race began with an accident that sent three cars spinning in the air. From the stand, Lil and Louis could see three men stretched out on the ground. Not believing it, Louis ran down to the track so that he could have a better view. He watched with disbelief as men with stretchers removed the mangled drivers from the track.

By the time he got back to where Lil was sitting, there was another incident. A man sitting on their side of the track started waving to someone on the other side. Lil and Louis watched in horror as the man started out across the track into the traffic, with racecars bearing down on him. The first two cars managed to miss him, but the third slammed straight into him, sending his body flying through the air. That was more than Lil and Louis could stand, so they left. Says Louis: "I told Lil, 'From now on I don't want to see a foot race let alone an automobile race.'"

For all the carnage they witnessed at the racetrack, they realized they could not keep going every place they needed to go in a taxi. They needed a car of their own, at least Lil thought so. Louis had no desire to learn to drive and he was not sure he wanted Lil to either. The only member of the band who had a car was Baby Dodds.

Sometimes Baby drove Lil and Louis where they needed to go in his Oldsmobile. Lil always sat in the front seat with Baby, and Louis sat in the back seat, and when Lil needed to talk to Louis, which was all the time, she turned around and leaned over the car seat with her back to the oncoming traffic.

Riding in Baby's car was not an ideal situation, either. For one thing, no one in the band was happy that he owned a car. He was a heavy drinker and everyone just knew he was going to get drunk and kill himself in that car.

Much to Louis's discomfort, Lil decided to buy her own car, a second-hand Hudson, one of the most popular cars of that era. According to Lil, it was "a block long and made a lot of noise like you were going ninety miles an hour when you are really going about thirty." Lil learned to drive away from Louis's prying eyes, and when she thought she was ready she invited both Louis and King Oliver to go for a ride in her new car. Of course, nothing went according to plan.

As she drove down Michigan Avenue, the motor went dead at the intersection of Thirty-Fifth Street and Michigan. Louis and Joe sat in the back seat laughing as the other motorists started honking their horns. Since neither of them knew anything about cars, they did not volunteer to give Lil a hand. Finally, one of the motorists got out of his car and showed Lil how to restart the motor. Said Lil: "I never could get [Louis and Joe] out riding again."[12]

King Oliver's Creole Jazz Band performed regularly at the Gardens until February 1923, at which time he decided to take the band on the road to do a tour in the Midwest. It was Louis's first time to leave Chicago and Lil's second. On one of their passes back through Chicago during that time, they were asked by the Starr Piano Company to do a recording session at the company's studio in Richmond, Indiana.

Oliver had been asked on other occasions to record his music, but he had always declined, thinking that it would be a mistake to trust anyone with his music. Although the phonograph had been around since the late 1870s, the recording industry was still in its infancy and the few musical records that were produced by the early 1920s featured vocalists, not instrumentalists, since the technology was only sufficient to reproduce three and one-half octaves of notes. That was fine for singers such as Enrico Caruso, who built a career around his recordings, but for musicians it did not offer much potential for either financial or creative success.

The Starr Piano Company was eager to subsidize recordings because it had an ownership interest in a phonograph company named Gennett, which also operated a successful record label named the Gennett Record Company. Starr sold the phonographs in its stores and used the phonograph records as a sales tool.

Gennett was not a major record label by any means, but it had achieved some success with recordings of the National Marimba Orchestra, recitations by William Jennings Bryan, and anti-black anthems sponsored by the Ku Klux Klan. Indiana was a strong-hold for the Klan in the 1920s, and it was well known throughout the black community.

Why Oliver accepted the offer to record there, knowing full well of the town's affiliation with the Klan, is a mystery, though it probably was based solely on financial considerations. The band was offered an advance on royalties and a promise of faithful accounting on record sales. There were no jazz records on the market, and the first blues records had been recorded only three years earlier by Mamie Smith.

On the morning of April 5, the entire band took the train from Chicago to Richmond. No one knew what to expect since none of them had ever made a record. Used to performing in large ball-rooms or outdoors, they were shocked to discover how small the studio was. The only good thing about the session was that they were allowed to choose their own music.

"Of course, everyone was on edge," says Baby. "We were all working hard and perspiration as big as a thumb dropped off us. Even Joe Oliver was nervous. . . . The only really smooth-working person there was Lil. She was very unconcerned and much at ease."

Gennett used a gramaphone to record the session. It was the best available technology at the time, but it was nonetheless a simple device. The band was asked to huddle around a large megaphone that collected the sound and transferred the sound waves to a wax-coated cylinder.

"We all had to blow in this great big horn, the old style," says Lil. "And in trying to get the balance, Joe and Louis stood right next to each other as they always had, and you couldn't hear a note that Joe was playing, only could hear Louis."[13]

To balance the music, they moved Louis about fifteen feet away from the band, over in a corner. He looked so pitiful, Lil felt sorry for him. Says Lil: "That's a bad sign when you start feeling sorry for a man, huh?"[14]

If Lil had any doubts about Louis's ability to play, the recording session quickly dissipated them. "I said to myself, 'Now if they have to put him that far away in order to hear Joe, he's got to be better.'"

King Oliver's Creole Jazz Band made history that day by making one of the very first jazz records. In all, they recorded nine tracks: "Just Gone," "Canal Street Blues," "Mandy Lee Blues," "I'm Going Away to Wear You Off My Mind," "Chimes Blues," "Weather Bird Rag," "Dippermouth Blues," "Froggie Moore," and "Snake Rag." The "Dippermouth Blues," composed by Oliver, is interesting because that was one of the nicknames the band called Louis.

They rode the train back to Chicago that night, not certain whether they had done a good thing or a bad thing. All they knew for certain was that they had a little more money in their pockets than they had when they made the train ride down to Indiana. Each band member was paid thirty dollars per song.

Not long after their return from Indiana, the Creole Jazz Band played an early morning engagement at the Drake Hotel, one of the city's finest. In the audience were talent scouts from Okeh Record Company, which had a studio in Chicago. Despite the late hour (around three o'clock), the band was mobbed by admirers that had gathered around the bandstand.

That was all it took for Okeh to offer the band a recording contract. Several weeks later, they went into the record label's West Washington Street studios and recorded several sides, many of them remakes of the songs they already had recorded for Gennett. Later that year, they also made recordings for Columbia and Paramount.

The African-American record market had become a lucrative business for the record companies. Not many whites purchased records by African-American artists at that time—they were politely advertised as "race" records—but they were so popular with blacks that it hardly mattered.

The records were sold everywhere that blacks gathered—in train stations, aboard the trains, on street corners, and in black-owned and -operated businesses. That racial exclusivity with jazz and blues records would change, but at the time the Creole Jazz Band made its first records, sales were targeted toward blacks.

If the record companies had asked them what they thought the market would be among white record buyers, the band most likely would have answered "excellent," because what they were seeing from the bandstand was a surge of interest among whites. The record companies never asked, so it took a while for them to figure it out.

Although individual band members were suspicious of the record companies—and Louis was hesitant to play his best stuff since he was afraid someone would steal it—the records did focus more attention on the band and allowed them to be more relaxed and confident when they performed.

When Lil saw how much of the band's newfound popularity was being focused on Louis, she encouraged him to improve his appearance. She urged him to lose weight. He did—fifty pounds. She talked him into throwing away his second-hand clothes. He did—under Lil's guidance he purchased a new wardrobe. She pleaded with him to be more assertive, to quit lurking in the background. He did that by stepping forward more often when he played, by singing an occasional song, by clowning around with a toy slide whistle, and by having more fun on the bandstand with the other players.

In addition to the little thing he always had going with Oliver, he developed a musical competition with Baby. Without warning, Louis would change tempo or improvise during a solo, challenging Baby to follow him on drums. Baby accepted each challenge with good humor, making a game out of it, which was not easy since whatever he did on his snare to keep up with Louis had to be separate from the steady beat of his bass drum, so as not to throw the other band members off rhythm. Says Baby: "Louis and I would throw each other [off] and pick it up ourselves and keep the band going."

Despite the good time they were having onstage, dissension began to build in the band over Oliver's control of the money. Sure, they were paid thirty dollars for each "side" they recorded in a recording studio, but they never saw any royalty statements as promised by the record labels. Was Oliver pocketing the money, or was the record label not paying any royalties?

Then they began to question whether Oliver was paying them as much as he should for their nightclub performances. Lil knew she was being paid more than Louis was being paid, and she could not help but wonder about that.

Lil urged Louis to stand up to Oliver, but he was hesitant. "Whenever Joe came to the house, you'd think that God walked in," says Lil. "Louis never seemed to be able to relax around him because he was so afraid of doing something that might upset him."[15]

Finally, Lil asked him the question she had been dying to ask, but had refrained from asking because she had feared offending Louis: "Where's your money, Louis?"

Louis told her that Joe was keeping it for him.

"Well, Joe doesn't get to keep your money. You keep your own money."

"Mr. Joe looks out for me," Louis responded.

"No," said Lil. "I'm going to look out for you now."

The very thought of Oliver keeping Louis's money made Lil angry. It was an old custom in the South, especially in Memphis where Lil grew up, for white employers to "hold onto" a black employer's wages and to issue them "spending money." Of course, on occasion more money was paid out to black employees for spending money and medical expenses than they had earned, but those times were rare. Oliver wasn't white, but he was playing the white man's game and Lil understood that game, even if she could not make Louis understand it.

"I'm going to get you some clothes and you're going to give me my money back," she told Louis. With that, she measured him with a tape measure went downtown to purchase him some new clothes. She bought him a gray overcoat and a twenty-dollar velour hat.[16] At work that night, everyone except Oliver complimented Louis on his new clothes. Oliver was angry. He told Louis that Lil was nothing but a spoiled kid and would spend all of his money.

"Yeah, I know," said Louis."[17]

Shortly after that, Louis went to Oliver for his money. Oliver had no choice but to give the money to Louis. But he was unhappy about it, and, perhaps as he feared, it set in motion a chain of events that would ultimately break up the band.

"Johnny Dodds found out that Joe had been collecting ninety-five dollars for each member of the band, while he had been paying us seventy-five," says Lil. "He had been making twenty dollars a week off of each of us for no telling how long. So Johnny and Baby Dodds, they threatened to beat Joe up. Joe brought his pistol every night to work in his trumpet case in case anything happened."[18]

Relationships in the music business are usually begun in friendship by individuals who share a common vision and passion. Those relationships are most often destroyed by the sworn enemy of all such relationships—questions about finances. Legendary record producer Chips Moman was fond of saying that the most interesting part of any music industry meeting was trying to determine who in the group was *not* a crook.

Once Baby and Johnny Dodds started asking Oliver questions about their paychecks, it marked the end of their relationship with the Creole Jazz Band, for Oliver had no adequate answers for why he was skimming money off the top of their accounts. The band members were also concerned because they had been promised royalties from their records and had thus far received no checks. In fairness to Oliver, that probably was not his fault since few record companies of that era bothered to pay black musicians anything past their initial advance.

Early in 1924, the Creole Jazz Band fell apart. Baby and Johnny Dodds left, and they were soon followed by everyone else except Lil and Louis. Lil wanted Louis to quit, but he still felt too much loyalty to Oliver to just walk away cold. Clarinetist Johnny Dodds got at job at a nightclub named Burt Kelly's Stables and soon brought Baby, Dutrey, and Bill Johnson into the group, which featured Freddie Keppard on trumpet.

"I felt awfully blue about seeing that band break up," says Baby. "I would forget it one minute and the next minute it was right back in my mind again. . . . It seemed as though something was missing from my life. It was pretty bad for a while."[19]

Lil and Louis reacted to the breakup of the band by drawing closer together. They had decided to get married late in 1923, but since they both were married at the time, there were certain legal niceties that had to be observed. Lil contacted a lawyer and arranged for both divorces. Louis's divorce was the last to be completed, and final papers were received two days before Christmas.

On February 5, 1924, Lil and Louis were married. Lil wore a white crepe gown that was decorated in rhinestones and silver beads. Her bridesmaid, Lucille Saunders, wore an orchid chiffon dress with silver trimmings. Music was supplied by Oscar Young's seven-piece orchestra.

Although Joe Oliver was opposed to the marriage, he attended with his wife, as did former Creole Jazz Band members Baby and Johnny Dodds. That evening, Lil and Louis went out on the town, hitting all the night spots. Everywhere they went that night people showered them with rice. There was so much rice, in fact, that when Louis looked back he saw a white carpet of rice on the ground that resembled snow.

Lil and Louis did not take a honeymoon. Instead, they went on tour with Oliver's reorganized band, but not before they bought a new home at 421 East Forty-Fourth Street. Dempsey moved into the home with them, which provided them with an extended family that consisted, at times, also of Louis's mother, Mayann, and his adopted son, Clarence.

Neither Lil nor Louis minded the crowded house. They were never there anyway, and it might have been a source of comfort for them to know that someone was at home taking care of business. Lil was twenty-six when they married, and Louis was twenty-three. For African Americans of that era, that was a very young age to be achieving the level of success they were experiencing. Louis had married the woman that every man in the band wanted, and Lil had married the man that every woman in Chicago wanted. They were jazz's first—and only—power couple.

Lil and Louis enjoyed their quiet evenings at home. After dinner, it was their custom to sit in the parlor, where Lil played the classics on a new baby grand piano Louis bought for her. In later years, Louis told the story of how Jelly Roll Morton and Louis's friend Zutty Singleton sometimes stopped by the house to play the piano, a Kimball.

That came as news to Lil, who in later years said, "I evidently wasn't at home that day, because I don't remember seeing them there." Of course, both recollections may be correct. Louis may have invited his friends over when Lil was out of the house.

Dempsey suffered a stroke shortly before their marriage and lost the use of one of her arms. As therapy, Louis bought her a secondhand typewriter. According to Louis, she became a pretty good one-handed typist and used the instrument to pass the time.

Mayann soon began to feel crowded in the house and decided she wanted to return to New Orleans. Truthfully, she had complained of missing the members of her old church congregation. The night before she left Chicago, Louis took her out on the town. They had such a good time that the police had to show them the way back home.

When Mayann returned to New Orleans, leaving Clarence behind to live with Louis, she did so with the knowledge that everyone was being well cared for, and that, after all, was the reason for her journey to Chicago in the first place.

One of the first people Mayann ran into upon her return was Louis's ex-wife, Daisy. When Mayann told her how well Louis was doing and how happy he was with his new wife, Daisy was shocked, for she had never been advised of the divorce. The proceedings had taken place in Chicago and apparently no effort had been made to serve her with notice of the divorce. Daisy was livid and vowed to do something about it.

In April 1924, Lil and Louis toured with Oliver's new band in Pennsylvania, Ohio, Michigan, and Wisconsin. They were on the road for most of the year. The new band was not nearly as good as the previous one, but Lil and Louis worked extra hard to pump life into it. "I danced, taken a lot of solos, you know, to help the old man out," says Louis. "After all, I was in there with him with all my heart because I loved Joe Oliver and would do anything in the world to make him happy."[20]

When they returned to Chicago, they resumed playing at the Gardens. No one was very happy with the new band, least of all Lil, who continued to urge Louis to quit. She felt Oliver was holding Louis back by keeping him on second trumpet and not allowing him to play more solos. Oliver was dictatorial that way.

Whenever Lil allowed her fingers to drift over to the upper end of the keyboard, Oliver always growled at her, "We've already got a clarinet." Oliver wanted her to play four-beats-to-the-measure rhythm. For all he cared, she could have played with her right hand in her pocket.

One night, shortly after their return to the Gardens, Louis was on the bandstand when he heard a disturbance at the front door. There was no doubt in his mind about who it was. He knew *that* voice. It was Daisy and she had run into trouble at the door because she said she was Mrs. Armstrong, and wanted to see her husband and the people at the door knew that Mrs. Armstrong was up on the bandstand performing with Louis.

Finally, as she bullied her way inside the door, shouting and shaking her fists, Louis was able to see her face. Knowing that she probably had a razor in her stocking, he left the bandstand to quiet her down. Together, they left the Garden and went to a nearby bar, where Louis told her about the divorce and his marriage to Lil.

Daisy was not too happy about the situation and kept saying that she loved Louis—that he, in fact, was the only man she would ever love—but Louis told her he was a changed man, that he was trying to cultivate himself and find a new life. That discourse went back and forth for some time, until Louis told her that he would "help her out" by doing everything within his power to see that she had the things that she needed. After hearing that he planned to slip her a little money from time to time, Daisy quieted down and said, "That's fair enough."

Daisy decided to stay in Chicago, no doubt to be near the source of Louis's money, and from time to time the two of them went out drinking. Louis never said in later years if they ever resumed their sexual relationship.

One night they were drinking in a bar when one of the patrons recognized Louis and made some disparaging comments about him. That so incensed Daisy that she confronted the man, informing him that she was Louis's wife and did not appreciate what he was saying about her husband.

As the argument grew more heated, the man pulled a knife and flashed it at Daisy. That was all she needed to get her hot blood pumping. Quick as a flash, she reached down into her stocking and pulled out her razor and barreled into the man, slashing and cutting with a fervor matched only by the man's determination to match her cut for cut with his knife. By the time the police and the ambulance arrived, both were cut pretty badly, with Daisy's worst cut located across her face.

It was incidents like that that kept Louis willing to shell out money to her. He was careful to keep Daisy away from Lil, and she apparently had no idea that Louis was keeping after-hours company with Daisy.

Not only was Louis caught between Lil and Daisy, he was caught between Lil and Oliver, and neither place was where he wanted to be. In his heart he knew Lil was right about Oliver. He had no future with him beyond what he already had, and ever since the band fell apart he had begun to wonder about his future.

Lil was his rock during this time.

Once they were married, Lil told him she didn't want to be married to a second trumpet. "What are you talking about?" he asked.

"Well, I don't want to be married to a second trumpet player. I want you to play first."

"I can't play first. Joe's playing first."

"That's why you've got to quit."

"I can't quit Mr. Joe. Mr. Joe sent for me and I can't quit him."

"Well, it's Mr. Joe or me!"

Louis asked what she wanted him to do. Give him notice, was her curt reply. But what about you, he asked—what are you going to do?[21]

"I'm going to stay," says Lil. "One of us needs to be working."[22]

Lil was right, of course. Oliver was holding Louis back—and he was doing it for selfish reasons. As far as jobs go, working on a regular basis with the Creole Jazz Band was about as good as it could get for an aspiring musician who had no grander vision. Lil saw things in Louis that no one else saw, with the possible exception of Oliver.

"I thought the best thing to do was to get him away from Joe," she told a writer for *Down Beat.* "I encouraged him to develop himself, which was all he needed. He's a fellow who didn't have much confidence in himself."

Louis was so self-effacing he did not grasp his own potential as a solo artist. One of the great mysteries of jazz is what Lil saw in him that others did not. In later years, after Louis had achieved stardom, there was no shortage of people to step forward and talk about the talent they recognized in those early years, but time has a way of amplifying memories like that. Those early recordings of Louis show an instrumentalist who was awfully good, but no better than King Oliver, Johnny Dodds, or Honore Dutrey.

"I would hear Louis coming home, whistling, for more than a block away," says Lil. "He had this most beautiful, shrill whistle and all those riffs that he later made in his music, he used to whistle. I thought, 'Maybe someday that guy will play like that.'"[23]

Louis may not have believed in himself, but he believed in Lil with all his heart. For a black woman to accomplish the things she had accomplished was unheard of at that time, especially in the South, a region that remained his point of reference for the rest of his life. If Lil could do for him half of what she had done for herself, then his possibilities must have seemed unlimited.

Louis handed in his resignation to Oliver, as Lil requested. That night, when Lil showed up for work at the Gardens as usual, Oliver pulled her aside to talk to her in private. "Louis gave me his notice," he said. "You didn't give me yours."

"No, I'm not quitting," Lil answered.

"Why did Louis quit?"

"I said, 'Well, you'll have to ask him,'" Lil later recalled to an interviewer, then laughed. "Such lies, huh?"

The next morning, Louis looked at Lil with a bewildered look on his face. "Now, what am I going to do?" he asked.

Lil told him to go out and look around and hang out with other musicians and find out who was looking for a new trumpet player. Louis did—every afternoon—but he didn't have much luck. Perhaps to please Lil, he targeted bands that had a reputation for being "society" orchestras.

The first one he approached was Sammy Stewart's orchestra. In the most unassuming manner possible, he asked Stewart if he could use a new horn man. Stewart turned around and snapped that he didn't need anyone, then turned his back on Louis to finish whatever he was doing. Stewart, a light-skinned African American, did not bother to explain to Louis that he was too dark to play in his Creole orchestra, so Louis naturally assumed he was rejected because of the way he played trumpet.

Disheartened, Louis returned home to Lil and told her what happened.

"Don't worry about him," says Lil. "Pretty soon he'll be eating at your feet."

Louis was stunned to encounter so much rejection. All the musicians and bandleaders that had stood in line at the Gardens to hear him play now seemed cool to the idea of hiring him for their bands. That possibility had never even occurred to him.

Then one day he heard that Ollie Powers was putting a band together to work in Dreamland. Wondering if he would remember the day he had tipped him one dollar to sing for him and Lil, Louis went to apply for a job and was pleasantly surprised when he was hired. No one was happier to hear the news than Lil, who was getting concerned but not sharing that concern with her husband for fear it would discourage him even more.

The best part of Louis's new job with Powers' band was the fact that he would be playing first trumpet. He was, in fact, the only trumpet on the bandstand. Within days, Louis was playing at Dreamland. One part of him was relieved to have a job, while the other part yearned for the good old days with Oliver, when he didn't have to think about anything except blowing his horn.

Despite his mixed feelings about playing with Powers, Lil saw a difference in his music right away. He played with more confidence, more passion.

Already a violent city when Lil arrived, Chicago had become a virtual battleground by the mid-1920s as Al Capone struggled first to consolidate his power, then to hold onto it as both rival gangs and the federal government worked to depose him. Before the decade ended, Capone would be credited with more than one hundred murders in Chicago. You could not be a musician in Chicago in the 1920s and not be affected by the mob, but aside from performing at mobsters' private parties, the only contact musicians had with the mob was through the nightclub owners and the grunts that served as intermediaries between the clubs and the mob bosses.

One Chicago resident who served in both capacities, clubowner and intermediary, was Joseph Glaser, a son of Russian-Jewish immigrants. His father was a physician, and he seemed headed in that direction as a young man until he slipped into the undertow of the Chicago mob. Fascinated by both the machinations of the underworld and the local music scene, he entered the "life" by accepting a job as the manager of the Sunset Café.

Glaser's brushes with the law began in the mid-1920s, when the Chicago *Tribune* identified him as part of a "gigantic conspiracy" to bribe policemen in connection with his duties at the Sunset. Judging by the company he kept—bootleggers and racketeers—it soon became apparent that he was fronting for the mob.[24] A string of arrests followed, beginning with a publicized raid in 1926 at the Sunset, where Glaser was charged with violating Prohibition. A year later he was convicted of running a whorehouse and fined one hundred dollars.

In addition to his legal difficulties, it soon became apparent that he was fighting personal demons. He was a pedophile who preyed on young girls, especially those he employed in his whorehouses. On June 22, 1927, Glaser was indicted for the rape of a fourteen-year-old child named Dolores Wheeler. It was at his trial that the public got its first glimpse of the part owner of the Sunset Café.

During the trial, it was disclosed that Glaser had been convicted of providing minor girls with alcohol and allowing them to perform "immoral" dances at the Sunset. Newspaper stories during the trial also pointed out that he was part owner of the

Plantation Café, along with Republican committeeman Ernest Potts and notorious gambler Billy Skidmore. Additionally, it was brought out that Glaser had signed numerous bonds for persons charged with various crimes, ranging from robbery to murder.

On February 7, 1928, Glaser was convicted of rape and sentenced to ten years imprisonment. When his attorney notified the judge of his intention to file an appeal, the judge set bond at fifteen thousand dollars, which Glaser paid. While awaiting the results of his appeal, Glaser made a deal with the child's stepfather, whereby they took her to Louisville, Kentucky, so that Glaser could marry her and hopefully beat the rap.

What Glaser wanted was the documentation of the marriage to present to the court. After the marriage, they sent her to Los Angeles so that authorities could not question her. That did not work, however, and she was returned to Chicago and committed to a private home. As a result of his efforts to facilitate the marriage, the stepfather was convicted of contempt of court and sentenced to six months in jail.

Meanwhile, Glaser's attorney alleged to the appeals court that the original indictment contained incorrect information. As it turned out, according to the records, the state had dismissed five of the six original counts of the indictment, leaving only the charge of forcible rape. The clerk who made the entries stated that he was given misinformation about the case. When asked who gave him the information, he said he did not recall. He said the mistake was unintentional.

As a result, the appeals court threw out the conviction, allowing Glaser to beat the rap. The Chicago Crime Commission did not agree that the error was unintentional: "It appears that someone probably paid some deputy clerk of the criminal court to falsify the record so that an appeal could be made on the grounds that evidence at the trial failed to substantiate the one charge of forcible rape."

Shortly after that, Glaser was arrested again, on much the same charges involving a seventeen-year-old girl. Again, his mob connections allowed him to beat the rap. A paternity suit followed in which another teenager charged him with being the father of her child. A variety of other charges followed, including conspiracy and receipt of stolen property, namely a liquor cargo valued at over two thousand dollars. The stolen property charge was dropped because of the refusal of witnesses to testify against Glaser. He pleaded guilty to the conspiracy charge, but was only fined fifty-six dollars.

Glaser's activities and scrapes with the law were well publicized at the time, but had no effect on the willingness of musicians to work in his nightclubs. Many felt safer working in mob-connected clubs than they did in legitimate venues. No one was shooting up the clubs that belonged to Glaser and those friendly to Capone.

The fear factor in the South Side during the Capone years was tremendous. It was not just that people were being killed on the streets of Chicago—it was *how* they were being killed. Through his use of the Thompson submachine gun, Capone brought a high-tech element of terror into his campaign to control the city.

First used in World War I by the U.S. Army, the submachine gun had the capacity to fire steel-jacketed 45-caliber bullets at a rate of six hundred per minute. That meant that gunmen could empty a one hundred-round clip within seconds. The "Tommy Gun," as it was called, gave Capone a distinct advantage over pistol-packing federal agents and police officers. The worst incident involving the Tommy Gun was the 1929 St. Valentine's Massacre, in which Capone gunmen mowed down six members of a rival gang in a Chicago garage. The grisly photographs of the bloody murders were carried in newspapers across the country.

African Americans figured that the violence that was going on was between the white people on the streets and the white people in the government. They did not see how it was any of their business to get mixed up in it. All they wanted out of it was the ability to make a living, especially if they were musicians, for any musician who ruled out working for the mob pretty much ruled out working, period.

After Louis left King Oliver's band and started working for Ollie Powers at the Dreamland, he and Lil presented a higher profile in the Chicago music community by going out to clubs and private parties as guests more often than they had done previously.

One private party that stuck out in Lil's mind in later years was hosted by a notorious bootlegger who invited musicians to get up and play with the band. Both Lil and Louis performed before the raucous crowd, but when Bessie Smith took the stage the bootlegger made it a point to hush the crowd before she sang. Lil theorized that he did it because Smith had such a volatile temper.

For the first time in their marriage, they were not with each other twenty-four hours a day. When he wasn't performing at Dreamland, Louis frequented the tougher mob-connected clubs such as the Sunset, where he got to know Joe Glaser. Lil did not approve of people like that, and he probably visited the seedier clubs without her knowledge, perhaps with Daisy who was still in town keeping an eye on Louis. He may have wanted Daisy with him because of her proficiency with a razor.

To Lil's disappointment, Louis was not entirely happy at Dreamland. He got to play plenty of solos, but his vaudeville-type humor seemed out of place with Ollie Powers. (Louis liked to do sight gags in which he fell down and picked himself back up, usually to the laughter of the customers.)

At that point in their lives, neither Louis nor Lil saw themselves as the creators of a new type of music. They played music because it paid better than anything else they could do and most of the time it was fun and exciting. Neither of them listened to or collected records. The creation of jazz was not an intellectual process for the couple; it was simply a byproduct of the lives they lived.

With Louis's departure, King Oliver decided to send to New Orleans for new players. When Louis heard about that, he started dropping hints to Lil that he might want to return to Oliver's band, where he could be himself and perform the humorous skits that gave him such enjoyment.

Before he was able to take that idea past the discussion phase, he received a telegram from Fletcher Henderson in New York. Fletcher wanted to know if Louis would be interested in joining his band, the Black Swan Troubadours. The timing of the telegram was serendipitous, perhaps an indication that Lil had contacted Henderson herself and offered Louis as a possible addition to his band.

Whether Henderson's invitation was chance or contrived, it arrived at the perfect moment. Both Lil and Louis were ready for an adventure.

"Struttin' With Some Barbecue"

Fletcher Henderson and Louis Armstrong had come a long way since their 1922 meeting in New Orleans. Only two years had passed, but for both men it seemed as if a lifetime of experiences had occurred during that interval.

Henderson's Black Swan Troubadours had a standing engagement at Roseland, one of New York City's top dance halls. In many respects, Henderson was a male version of Lil. He came from middle-class beginnings in Atlanta, Georgia, where his family had sacrificed to educate him in the ways of polite white society. He dressed well, spoke well, and considered himself above the black rabble that Louis liked to rub elbows with at the after-hours clubs in Chicago. He even possessed a college degree in chemistry.

When Henderson left Atlanta to go to New York in 1920, it was not to form a band but to pursue an advanced degree in chemistry at Columbia University. Those plans fell through when he ran out of money and took a job selling songs for W. C. Handy to support himself. That led to a position as an accompanist at Black Swan

Records, where he played piano for some of their recording acts such as Ethel Waters.

By 1923, he was heading up his own orchestra, the other players having elected him leader because of his light skin and good manners. The following year, he got his first big break when his orchestra was given the Roseland booking. There was only one problem: only weeks before the engagement began, Henderson's first chair cornet player, Joe Smith, left to take a booking with a Broadway play. It was at that point that Louis entered the picture.

Louis went to New York alone, leaving Lil behind to pack and put their affairs in order before joining him in two weeks. Louis had lived his entire life in cities, but he was ill prepared for what greeted him in New York. Chicago had several upscale clubs, but most were bootleggers' dives. Chicago's black community lived in poverty, much as it did in New Orleans. New York had the same pockets of poverty, but it also had uptown sophistication and grandeur amid tree-lined boulevards.

Louis would never forget his first day of work with Henderson's orchestra—and neither would they, for they saw a timid, poorly dressed squat little man whose extra weight was bursting out of his suit in all the wrong places.

Louis arrived at Roseland while the band was in rehearsal. He introduced himself and offered his hand to Henderson. "He could see I was a wee bit frightened, his band being the first big-time orchestra I had the pleasure of joining," says Louis.[1]

"So you're Louis Armstrong?'

"Yassuh," answered Louis.

"Your part is up on the bandstand."

Louis took his place on the bandstand, where he found the sheet music for the third trumpet part (Lil had taught him how to read music by that time). What he remembered most about that day was how quiet the band was as he took his place among them.

No one said anything; they just stared at him. The first arrangement they played was "By the Waters of Minnetonka."

Louis went by the book for the first week or so. Then, when he could stand it no longer, he started airing out his horn the way he liked to do in Chicago. The band members all stared at him when he played like that, but this time it was a good look, one that told him that they approved of the way he played.

Lil joined Louis in New York, but was disappointed to discover that her reputation had not preceded her. In Chicago everyone who was anyone of importance knew about "Hot Miss Lil." That wasn't the case in New York, where the notion of a woman playing blues and jazz piano with a male orchestra seemed laughable.

W. C. Handy had brought orchestration to the blues—and that had found wide acceptance in New York—but the type of music that Lil played in Chicago seemed raw and uncouth by New York standards, a realization that must have shocked her in view of the exalted position she held in Chicago.

By contrast, Louis's reputation grew each day, especially among the other musicians in the city. Cornet player Rex Stewart almost couldn't believe his own eyes and ears. He went into Roseland, time after time, to listen to Louis. "I went mad with the rest of the town," he explained. "I tried to walk like him, talk like him, eat like him, sleep like him. Finally, I got to shake hands and talk with him."[2]

What Lil and Louis discovered in New York was a world they had only seen glimpses of in Chicago. Two years before their arrival in the city, F. Scott Fitzgerald had published a book titled *Tales of the Jazz Age*. Of course, what Fitzgerald and the rest of America called jazz was really the blues as orchestrated by W. C. Handy. When Fitzgerald wrote about the Jazz Age, his focus was not on the music but on the excesses of Prohibition and the extravagant lifestyles that defined the era for those in their twenties. Creatively, it was one of the most remarkable times in American history.

As Lil and Louis were inventing jazz, literary contemporaries such as Fitzgerald, Ernest Hemingway, and William Faulkner were exploring the perimeters of race relations, the American Dream, and the morality of previous generations. On the surface, the Jazz Age was about gin, flappers, and abundant wealth; it was what was beneath the surface that would have a more profound impact on American culture.

Shortly after Louis and Lil arrived in New York, Henderson sent to Chicago for saxophonist Buster Bailey. Louis was happy to see another midwesterner arrive, but he was annoyed at the reason Henderson wanted Bailey, which was to add another solo instrument to the group. Despite an uncertain beginning, the two men became good friends and discovered they shared a fondness for Chicago.

Despite stiff competition from Bailey, Louis quickly emerged as the orchestra's main soloist—and he did so by breaking the rules. Instead of merely following the melody, which was the style at that time, he broke away with countermelodies and altered time signatures, so that he often seemed to be playing in a parallel universe. No one really understood what he was doing, but he did it so well that it captivated other band members as well as the audience.

Once Henderson's band began recording, Louis's importance to the group became even more apparent as his sparkling solos dominated every song on which he appeared. Soon he was asked to perform on the records of others.

In November 1924, Louis and Lil were asked to participate in a recording session with Alberta Hunter. The studio band, named the Red Onion Jazz Babies, featured Louis on cornet, Lil on piano, Buster Bailey on clarinet, Aaron Thompson on trombone, and

Buddy Christian on banjo. They recorded several songs with Hunter, including "Everybody Loves My Baby," "Nobody Knows the Way I Feel Dis Mornin'," and "Cake Walking Babies."

Despite Louis's growing star status in New York, Henderson made no effort to single him out for special recognition, an oversight that rankled Lil to no end. She felt Henderson should use Louis's name in the orchestra's billing. He was the star, after all.

Not surprisingly, Lil decided to return to Chicago.

Late in 1925, Lil took the train to New York to visit Louis. She was unhappy with what she saw. He was falling into the same type of relationship with Henderson that he had with Oliver, which is to say he was allowing him to take unfair advantage of his talent. Lil had this vision of Louis being the greatest trumpet player in the world, and whenever he settled for a lesser vision it disturbed her. She wondered if she was the only person in the world who could see what lay ahead for Louis.

When she ended her visit, it was with a purpose.

"Well, you're situated all right," she told Louis. "I'm going back to Chicago."

The first thing Lil did after returning home was to go by Dreamland.

"I want to put a band in," she told the manager.

"Who you got?"

"Well, I've got some good musicians, but I want to bring my husband back from New York," she said, adding that she wanted him to be featured on the marquee and to receive seventy-five dollars a week, more than the fifty-five-dollars-a-week he was getting in New York. The manager told her she was crazy.

"Never mind," said Lil. "They know me, and they'll come in."[3]

Reluctantly, the manager agreed. Per Lil's instructions, he made up a sign that read: LOUIS ARMSTRONG—THE WORLD'S GREATEST TRUMPET PLAYER.

Once she had made all the arrangements, Lil wrote to Louis and told him it was time to come home. It had turned out to be a busy year for Louis. In addition to performing and recording with Henderson's orchestra, he was asked to play on several records made by Bessie Smith. It was an inspired pairing, for they both approached music with the same mindset. Smith would show up at the session with the idea for a song in her head and she would sing a few lines, and Louis would fill in the empty spaces with his horn. One of their strongest collaborations occurred on Handy's "St. Louis Blues."

After a six-month continuous engagement at Roseland, Henderson took the orchestra on the road, primarily in New England. They set up headquarters in Lawrence, Massachusetts, where they spent the summer of 1925 performing for dances in surrounding towns. In their off-hours they went swimming in a nearby river.

Before leaving New York, Louis had begun an affair with a woman named Fanny Cotton. She visited him several times while he was in Massachusetts, and Louis promised her that he would marry her as soon as he was free to do so. He tried to keep it a secret, but word eventually got out. Lil never discussed Fanny in later years, but it is entirely possible she knew about the relationship. It may have been what instigated her demand that he return to Chicago.

When the orchestra returned to New York at the end of the summer and picked up where they had left off at Roseland, Louis discovered that Fanny had left town. When Louis got Lil's letter, he knew it was time to leave New York. She had been hinting that maybe it was time for him to quit Henderson's band for quite some time, but he always managed to sweet talk another tour out of her, usually with the argument that they needed the money.

"I wrote and told him, 'Well, you can give Fletcher your two weeks' notice and come on back home—you'll get seventy-five dollars a week," says Lil. "He didn't believe me, and he didn't want to leave. He kind of liked playing with Fletcher. He was anxious to be a star. He just liked playing, and he thought I was crazy with all that name stuff, putting his name out there."

Louis said he wanted to stay in New York. Irritated, Lil told him that if he was not back by a certain date, he could just stay in New York, for all she cared—and never return to Chicago. This time Louis knew he had no choice.

"I had to choose between my wife and Fletcher's band," Louis said. "I chose being with my wife."[4] It was not a very difficult choice. "I stayed and tolerated those fellows [for two years] and their cutting up on the bandstand, instead of playing their music right," says Louis, who gave Henderson two weeks' notice.[5] "Oh, I was so relieved and happy over that. The fellows in Fletcher's band had such big heads. . . . [Henderson] only let me play third cornet in his band the whole time I was in his band. He'd only give me sixteen bars, at the most, to get off."

The bandleader told him that if he ever changed his mind, he would always have a place open for him in his band. The day after receiving Lil's letter he sent her a telegram that read simply, "I will be there."

Two weeks later, when he arrived in Chicago he found that Lil had been busy. She had put together an eight-piece band named Lil's Dreamland Syncopators, for which Louis would play lead trumpet. When he questioned that he would really be receiving seventy-five dollars a week, she showed him the contract. He was astonished. He didn't know another musician who made that kind of money. Then Lil took him by the club so that he could see his name on the marquee. He was appalled.

"What do you mean calling me the world's greatest trumpet player?" he said.

Ever the behind-the-scenes manipulator, Lil had also arranged for an advertisement in the Chicago *Defender* that announced the return of the "world's greatest trumpet player" to Chicago. Still almost pathologically shy, Louis was humiliated by all the attention. His greatest fear was that the other musicians in town would laugh at him and think he was boastful. No one laughed. By that time, Louis really was the greatest trumpet player in the world.

Lil also showed him the papers for the house she had purchased in both their names. He was elated, but thought it was too good to be true. Lil and Dempsey were still caring for Clarence, and it meant a lot to Louis for him to have a real home.

"Really, is this our house?" he asked, the emphasis on "our."

Lil laughed: "Well, someday it will be our house."

Not long after he started working for Lil at Dreamland, Louis got an offer from Erskine Tate to join his symphony orchestra at the Vendome Theatre. Originally built as a dance hall before the turn of the century, the Vendome had been remodeled by 1925 into an upscale movie theater. Tate's orchestra performed during the movie and at intermission. Working there was considered a step up from nightclubs, so when Louis received the offer he was so ecstatic he "liked to have fainted."

Lil agreed with him that it was a good opportunity, and they worked out an arrangement so that Louis could perform both at the Vendome and at Dreamland with Lil's band. Louis later recalled the opening night at the Vendome as being "sensational."

It didn't take long for Louis himself to be recognized as "sensational," especially on Sundays, when each band member was given the opportunity to play solo on a feature tune. "He made a high F on the end [of some songs]," says Lil. "So, you know people would come to two and three shows to see if he would miss that high F. He never missed it, but he started worrying [about it]."[6]

She advised him to come home and make some "G's."

Louis took her advice and sat around the house for days playing his trumpet, hitting one high G after another. Lil had learned long ago that it was not enough to simply *tell* Louis what he should do in his career. She had to *show* him how to find out for himself. "Psychologically, I was right," she later admitted. "If you can get a G at home, then you don't worry about an F at the theater."[7]

Lil was not only brilliant as a musician, she was skilled as an amateur psychologist, especially when dealing with men. She grew up in a household dominated by a strong, ambitious woman, and it is not surprising that Lil would turn out to be the head of a matriarchal household. She used psychology on Louis whenever possible, but when that failed she did not hesitate to use verbal admonishments.

Lil and Louis had an unusual marriage. The only marriage that compares to it, at least in the public arena, is the one forged years later by former President Bill Clinton and his wife, Hillary. It was a marriage characterized by love and affection, convenience, mutual career goals, and sexual experimentation.

Louis fooled no one with his "secret" affairs with Daisy and Fanny, least of all Lil. But as long as the affairs did not threaten the stability of the family unit—and that included Dempsey and Clarence—they were allowed to continue. Above all else, Lil was a pragmatist.

Lil's biggest test to date would occur over a nineteen-year-old woman Louis met while working at the Vendome. Her name was Alpha Smith, and in the beginning she was little more than a face in the crowd. One side effect of Louis's raised profile at the Vendome was the attention he attracted during his solos, when he played the audience for laughs as well as musical appreciation. The young girls loved the slapstick comedy he threw in whenever possible, and in no time he acquired his own contingent of groupies.

The affair began as a flirtation, with Alpha sitting on the front row so that she could flirt with Louis during his performances. Louis flirted right back, unless, of course, Lil was in the audience. It was a game to him, until they started meeting after the show; then it turned into a passionate sexual relationship.

Louis justified his infidelity by charging that Lil was having an affair of her own with a "pimp" she had met at Dreamland. It is possible that Lil was having an affair, but not likely since sex was never a driving force in her life, not even with Louis.

Louis and Alpha didn't meet in the clubs often because too many people knew him and he was afraid word would get back to Lil. Since Alpha worked as a babysitter for a white couple in Hyde Park named Mr. and Mrs. Taylor, they sometimes met at the couple's home in the afternoon and in the evening. One night, the couple arrived home earlier than expected and discovered Louis and Alpha in the parlor, where they were playing records, dancing, and sipping the couple's finest whiskey.

"Mr. and Mrs. Taylor, I want you to meet my new boyfriend—his name is Louis Armstrong," said Alpha. "He's the cornet player in Erskine Tate's orchestra down at the Vendome Theater."[8]

To Louis's relief, the Taylors responded in a friendly manner. He later learned that the Taylors had been unhappy with some of Alpha's previous boyfriends and were pleased to see her dating someone of substance, even if he was a married man. Later, Alpha took him to her mother's house to meet her family. Louis liked Alpha's mother, especially the way she told jokes and made him laugh.

Louis rationalized his infidelity with Alpha by blaming it on Lil. "Lil and I had one of the finest homes in Chicago at the time I was 'sweethearting' with Alpha," says Louis. "But still with all of that swell home Lil and I had, there was not happiness there. We were always fussing and threatening to break up if I sat on the bed after it was made up. Why, Lil would almost go into fits, and poor Clarence my adopted son with his nervous self used to almost jump out of his skin when Lil or Lil's mother would holler at him. . . . Whenever they, especially Lil, would holler at me I'd tell her just where to do. I'd say, 'Aw, woman—Go to hell!' "9

On November 12, 1925, Lil and Louis went into a recording studio together for the first time since the recording sessions with King Oliver. It happened almost by accident. Lil had heard that Okeh Records was looking for some musicians to record a few sides, and she talked them into asking Louis to front a band for the recording sessions. There were no grand expectations on either side. The musicians would be paid fifty dollars each for the session.

It was at times like this that Lil's genius came to light. Louis was the incomparable leader on the bandstand, especially when he played his horn. Lil was the leader when it came to taking care of all the business that got him on the bandstand.

First came the task of putting together the band. That was easy. Lil called in the musicians she and Louis both had played with in bands around town. There was Kid Ory on trombone, Johnny Dobbs on clarinet, Johnny St. Cyr on banjo, and, of course, Lil on piano and Louis on trumpet. There were no drums at this point; the rhythm would derive from the piano and the banjo. The band had to have a name, so Lil chose Louis Armstrong and the Hot Fives, obviously a derivative of the "Hot Miss Lil" title she had chosen for herself early in her career.

Okeh Records did not tell them what to record, but Lil understood the importance of a band doing original songs. She had been writing and copyrighting songs since 1920. For this session, she brought four songs: "My Heart," a revamped version of a song she had copyrighted in July 1920; "My Heart Will Always Lead Me Back to You"; "(Yes) I'm in the Barrel"; and one song composed by Louis for the session, "Gut Bucket Blues." Before going into the studio, the band rehearsed the songs so that they would be prepared when the wax spindle started turning.

Of all the band members, only Lil could see beyond the session. She understood all about song royalties and the value of having Louis's name identified with new songs that had not previously been recorded.

The session went off without a hitch. "My Heart" was originally written as a waltz, but by the time Louis and the band got through with it, it was a swinging four-beats-to-a-bar jazz original. Each band member took turns offering a solo, but Louis never overpowered any of them, preferring instead to weave his magic in and out of the musical path followed by the others. Louis's evocative tones were fluid and mellow, and Lil's piano playing, except for a ragtime-like solo, was steady and squared in the center of the keyboard, just the way King Oliver had always instructed her.

"(Yes) I'm in the Barrel" begins with a somber funeral march of the type that Louis played often in New Orleans, then breaks into a free-for-all with the trombone punctuating the piano and banjo, leaving Louis and Dodds to play off each other like two cats batting a ball of twine back and forth. Louis's final solo is sheer magic.

"Gut Bucket Blues," named after the container used to hold body parts removed from chickens, hogs, and wild game, introduces Louis's voice for the first time as he talks the other musicians in and out of their solos. The song begins with a driving banjo riff that would later be adapted by rock 'n' roll guitarists as a standard opening to hundreds of songs. Midway through, Lil offers up an energetic, twelve-bar solo that must have sent her ninety-pound body rocking. By the time Dodds and Ory do their solos you are left thinking it cannot possibly get any better. Then, of course, Louis wraps it up with notes that are so round and full that you think you've entered another dimension.

When they finished the session, they each collected their fifty dollars and went their separate ways, except for Lil and Louis. They were a true band in name only, since each player worked nightly with other musicians. For them it was a good day's pay for a good day's work. For everyone else, it was musical history.

It was the first true jazz session ever recorded—not the ragtime that entertained F. Scott Fitzgerald and his flappers, but a new music that would someday be recognized as one of America's most important cultural contributions to the world.

As Lil's recording career with Louis blossomed, her marriage shriveled, slowly disintegrating, week by week, month by month, as methodically as leaves fall from a tree. She loved Louis more than she had ever loved a man and more than she ever would love a man again, but that love would not allow her to submit to Louis's whims and idiosyncrasies, especially when she knew they were wrong-headed.

Louis continued his romance with Alpha, basking in the glow of her admiration. Louis had needs that often seemed conflicting. He needed a woman who could be strong and keep him on track, as his mother and Daisy and Lil had done so effectively; but as much as he needed that type of relationship he invariably resented it. Instead of blaming himself for needing what they offered, he blamed them for giving him what he needed.

Louis possessed a strong concept of honor and fidelity, but he applied it only to his male friends and employers. Psychologically, he was incapable of applying that same standard to the women in his life. Lil was just the opposite. She did not recognize a difference between men and women, not when it came to moral and ethical capability. Dempsey had ingrained a strong sense of right and wrong in Lil, not just the biblical kind, but the cultural kind, the compass that had allowed her mother and her mother before her to break the bonds of slavery.

The main difference between Lil and Louis was that Louis and his family had never progressed beyond the minimum standards of slavery. In his heart, Louis felt he *was* a slave of the white culture and would never escape that bondage. Lil knew better—and when she scolded him, when she nettled him about his manners or his bad habits, it was done with a view of freeing him from the bondage of his past.

Some part of Louis knew that was the case, and he understood that everything that Lil did for him she did for the right reasons, but the unfreed slave inside yearned for the simple emotional reinforcements of women like Alpha, who was too young to know enough about life to make suggestions to Louis about what he should and should not do.

Alpha was a warm body that embraced him when he was weak and confused, as his mother had done when he was a child. She praised his sense of humor, she complimented him on the way he dressed, and she made it clear that he was the undisputed king of their intimate world.

Throughout the latter part of 1925, Louis escalated his relationship with Alpha by taking Clarence with him to visit the family. Louis considered Alpha's mother to be part of the deal. Both women doted over him and made him feel special. He took Clarence to visit them because he wanted to see if they reacted the same way toward his adopted son.

The initial meeting was such a success that Clarence asked Louis if he could move in with Alpha and her mother. That was all

National Guardsmen are called out to quell race riots in Chicago in July 1919. (*Hulton Getty/Archive Photos.*)

The Hot Five (left to right): Johnny Dodds, Louis Armstrong, Johnny St. Cyr, Kid Ory, and Lil Hardin Armstrong. (*Frank Driggs Collection/Archive Photos.*)

Lil Hardin Armstrong in her bandleader's gown (circa 1930s). (*Frank Driggs/ Archive Photos.*)

Lil Armstrong at the piano. (*Louis Armstrong House and Archives, Queens College, CUNY.*)

Lil Armstrong in a rare publicity photo. (*Louis Armstrong House and Archives, Queens College, CUNY.*)

Louis needed to spur him into action. He packed up Clarence's belongings and moved him into the Smith household. He also moved himself in, though there was no discussion with Lil about a legal separation. He continued his relationship with Lil, the main difference being that he spent more nights at the Smith household.

Certainly, Lil's working relationship with Louis continued unabated. On February 26, 1926, Louis Armstrong and the Hot Fives returned to Okeh's Chicago studio for their second recording session. The way that worked, Okeh told them how many songs they wanted to record and Lil and Louis wrote or gathered the required number of songs and rehearsed them with the band. For this session, Lil contributed only one song, "You're Next," but she worked with Louis on one of his songs (he would play the songs and she would write it down in musical notation as he played).

"Cornet Chop Suey" was written by Louis several years earlier and copyrighted for him by Lil in 1924. The song opens with a flourish from Louis and is filled with the stops and fluid breaks that only he could do so well. On the bridge, Lil plays a full chorus solo, rather stiffly, but the song keeps building until the coda, when Louis explodes into a big finish. The song had nothing to do with Chinese food; the title was Louis's way of paying tribute to a dish of which he was inordinately fond.

"You're Next" began with Lil on piano and continued at a slow, bluesy tempo, with Louis leading the way for Dodds on clarinet and Kid Ory on trombone. It was followed by Ory's "Muskrat Ramble," a song that ultimately became a classic, though it was never recorded as effectively as it was on that day. Other songs included "Come Back, Sweet Papa," on which Dodds doubled on alto saxophone, and "Oriental Strut."

Lil was the star of "Georgia Grind," sharing the vocal with Louis. The song was almost entirely composed of vocals against a banjo rhythm, except at the very end, when the entire band joined in with a flourish.

The highlight of the session was "Heebie Jeebies," a song that called for a vocal from Louis. He sang it as planned, then halfway through the vocal he began "scatting," which is to say he sang nonsense words and syllables that followed the intonation of his trumpet. The song made music history by becoming the first scat recording.

Louis would build on that technique for the remainder of his life, as did scores of other recording artists, everyone from Billie Holiday to Bing Crosby. Later, when asked why he started scatting on the song, Louis claimed he did it because the sheet music fell off the stand and he had to do *something.* Lil never disputed that.

Lil and Louis's vocals sounded tinny, as if they were shouting up from the bottom of a well, but that was due to the technical limitations under which they worked. There were no microphones, no mixing boards, no electronic gauges that told them when the music was not balanced. As they had done in Indiana, they played and sang into a horn that was attached to the recording machine. Johnny St. Cyr sat on top of a small ladder to get the proper distance from the microphone for his banjo.

None of that mattered when the records were released, however. Louis Armstrong and the Hot Fives were the talk of Chicago. Within weeks of release, "Heebie Jeebies" sold over forty thousand copies. No one was sure what the phrase meant, but everyone started using it. In time, saying someone gave you the "heebie jeebies" was synonymous to saying they gave you the creeps. What began in Chicago as a local phenomenon soon spread across the nation. Louis was a star, and Lil was a star-maker.

Early in 1926 Louis left his job at the Vendome. With all the fame he was getting from his records, it just didn't seem right to be squandering it by playing in an orchestra pit for silent movies.

He continued on for a few months at Dreamland, but by spring he was ready to leave Lil's band, primarily because of their strained personal relationship.

King Oliver had formed another band, and for a while Louis considered rejoining his group at the Plantation Cafe. He did not because Lil was so opposed to it. Instead, he joined the Carroll Dickerson band at the Sunset Café. Lil did not like that either, primarily because owner Joe Glaser had such a bad reputation, but her influence with Louis was not strong enough to back him away from *two* bands of his choice.

Billed as "Chicago's Brightest Pleasure Spot," the Sunset Café had become by 1926 the city's premier nightclub. Everyone knew about the mob's association with the club and everyone knew about Glaser's legal problems involving young girls, but the times were such that no one really cared what Glaser did in private or with whom he associated in his business dealings. Chicago wanted to have a good time, and the Sunset Café was the best place in town to do that.

"I always admired Mr. Glaser from the first day I started working for him," says Louis. "He just impressed me different than the other bosses I've worked for. He seemed to understand colored people so much, and he was wonderful to his whole show and band."[10]

Armstrong loved working at the Sunset Café. It catered to a racially mixed audience, providing Louis with the best of two worlds. Al Capone was a frequent visitor and Louis was impressed by his interest in music. Because of his expansive smile and sometimes ingratiating voice, Louis was perceived to be something he was not. There was a dark side to Louis, one that thrived on the excitement of violence and deceit. He enjoyed the company of tough men and loose women. The Sunset Café was the perfect place for him to work, all the more so since it was well away from Lil's prying eyes.

Louis had not worked at the Sunset Café for long when Glaser pushed Dickerson aside and renamed the band Louis Armstrong and His Stompers. Glaser elevated Dickerson's piano player, Earl Hines, to the title of musical director, setting in motion a long-standing competition and friendship between Louis and Hines. The piano player was so good that whatever Louis played on his trumpet, Hines mimicked on piano. It was exactly the sort of give-and-take competition that always got Louis's creative juices flowing.

With Louis no longer a member of Lil's band at Dreamland, she reorganized it to suit her interests, not Louis's. "For a small unit they can't be beat, and they play a whole lot better than some of the 'star' cabaret bands," said a newspaper story. "Their rendition of jazz is pleasing, not that vulgar, mushy kind that invites immoral dancing, and it is well for the place, as it keeps an atmosphere of class in the place."

That last observation was obviously a reference to the perceived decadence of clubs like the Sunset Café. Although Louis was living a double life, with two different families, Lil stayed on course, standing by her principles as fervently as Louis strayed from her bedroom and her moralistic view of life.

Everyone in the music community knew about their strained relationship, and those musicians who resented Lil's influence on Louis and her boldness at venturing where women had previously not ventured criticized Lil at every opportunity, often telling Louis that he was henpecked. When that happened, Louis defended himself by defending Lil.

"I listened very careful when Lil told me to always play the lead," says Louis. "Play second trumpet to no one. They don't come great enough [to outplay him], and she proved it. Yes sir, she proved that she was right. You're damned right she did. The guys who called me henpecked all the time, they were broke all the time and I always had a pocketful of money. I had everything I wanted and the best. Them suckers got their ragged and a bowl of salt trying to give me hell. I'm sharp as a wedding dick."[11]

The way Lil and Louis treated each other at the recording sessions, you would never have known anything was wrong in their relationship. The next recording dates with Okeh were on June 16 and June 23, 1926. This time they went into the studio with eight songs. The lineup for the band was the same, except for the addition of Clarence Babcock, who was brought in to do vocals on two songs. Becoming quite the prolific writer, Lil took four new songs to the two sessions: "I'm Gonna Gitcha," "Droppin' Shucks," "King of the Zulus," and "Lonesome Blues."

With "I'm Gonna Gitcha," Lil gave Louis the formula that would eventually make him a superstar: an introduction that allowed him to play his trademark crystal-clear notes, following in the last third of the song with a scratchy vocal that stood out in stark contrast to his horn voice.

Lil understood what few others did: as much as he loved to turn heads with his skill on the trumpet, Louis's secret passion was to become a minstrel-type entertainer who could make people laugh as well as dance. *Those* were the people who were rich and famous, not horn players. Who had ever heard of a horn player becoming famous simply by playing his instrument?

"King of the Zulus" has been dismissed by jazz purists as a novelty tune, but to do so is to really miss the point of what Lil and Louis were attempting to do with their music. The couple were collaborators on many of the songs that each copyrighted under their individual names. Louis heard melodies in his head, and Lil translated those melodies into a structured framework with appropriate rhythms. In many respects, they were the John Lennon and Paul McCartney of the Jazz Age.

What they attempted to do with "King of the Zulus" was the same thing that Lennon and McCartney attempted with "Sgt. Pepper's

Lonely Hearts Club Band." The latter was no more rock 'n' roll than "King of the Zulus" was jazz, but both are great songs because they create theatrical images that entice the listener into thought and emotion not derived entirely from the music itself. Both songs would feel more at home on a Broadway stage than on a jukebox.

"King of the Zulus" begins with march-like rhythms and stops, followed by a somber but sultry trombone solo by Ory. Midway through the song Babcock interrupts the music by speaking in a faux Jamaican accent extolling the culinary benefit of soul food. As usual, Louis plays his solo with passion, occasionally hitting the high notes for which he later would become famous.

Cornetist Rex Stewart, who would later become one of Duke Ellington's stars, was a contemporary of Louis's. Better than anyone else, he explained the importance of those high notes. "Back in the twenties, the acceptable high-note range for the trumpet was high C, and to hit or play over C made the player exceptional," he wrote. "That is until Louis came along with his strong chops, ending choruses on F. We guys strained might and main to emulate him but missed most of the time. . . . Lots of guys ruined their lips and their career trying to play like [Louis]."[12]

"Droppin' Shucks" seems to begin in mid-chorus. After a piano solo by Lil, it blends into one of Louis's raspy vocals that tell a story about infidelity and romantic revenge. The melody is distinct and memorable, and it may have originated with Louis's compulsive whistling.

Lil begins "Lonesome Blues" on the piano, bolstered by Dodds's soulful clarinet, then Louis kicks in with a vocal that is more mellow than any others he had done to date. They lyrics tell the story of a man who is lonesome for his sweetheart; Lil obviously wrote the lyrics to express her own loneliness over Louis's absences to be with Alpha. Louis seemed genuinely touched when he sang the lyrics, for he knew he was singing Lil's feelings about him.

After they finished the session, they participated in a concert at the Coliseum staged by Okeh Records. The idea was to promote the company's entire roster, including in addition to the Hot Fives, Erskine Tate, and King Oliver. More than ten thousand people turned out for the concert. It was the only public performance ever made by the Hot Fives, and according to press reports the highlight of the evening was Louis's solo on "Cornet Chop Suey."

The Hot Fives was one of the most successful jazz bands in history, yet it existed only in the studio, brought together by Lil's musical vision and wifely determination. Lil was not the most talented musician in the group session, but she and her songs were the catalyst that allowed the magic to take place.

Lil allowed the group to be promoted as "Louis Armstrong and The Hot Fives," but the group was her creation, not Louis's. In later years, she often expressed astonishment that people put so much emphasis on the group. "We had no idea in the beginning that jazz was going to be that important, that someday people would want to know how we started, what we did, what records we made, and it's amusing to read in books people tell why we did this," she said. "I'm glad they know, because we didn't."[13]

In between recording sessions, Lil continued to perform at Dreamland and other clubs, but she began looking for ways to improve herself. To her, music was a means to an end, not the sole reason for her existence.

Always sorry that she had left Fisk University before receiving a degree—especially since she told people that she had—she looked for ways to continue her education. With that in mind, she enrolled in the Chicago College of Music.

While Lil worked to expand her mind, Louis continued performing at the Sunset Café. He felt secure in the company of strong men like Capone and Glaser. Just as Alpha boosted his male ego, so did the praise of Chicago's real bosses. It was during this time that he began to expand his own mind, though certainly not in a way that would have been approved by Lil: he started smoking marijuana.

It began innocently enough, with Louis sharing cigarettes with the underworld crowd at the Sunset Café. Addiction did not take long, and soon he was smoking it every day, progressing to the point where cigarettes were not enough. The more he smoked, the more he needed to smoke. Eventually, it got to the point where his daily "cigarettes" expanded into big, thick, cigar-sized joints.

"When I picked up my first stick of gage [Louis's word for marijuana] . . . I had myself a ball," he later wrote. "That's why it really puzzles me to see marijuana connected with narcotics, dope, and all that kind of crap."

The drug never impressed him as dope, he explained, because he recalled his mother and "church sisters" picking weeds similar to marijuana along the railroad tracks. "They would bring it to their homes, get a big fat slice of salt meat—and make the most dee-licious pot of greens."[14]

The illegality of the drug never seemed an issue with Louis, primarily because marijuana was not the only illegal substance at the Sunset Café—almost *everything* that happened in the club was illegal, except for the music.

Illegal alcohol was served in the club, illegal weapons were in evidence, illicit romances between whites and blacks were commonplace (certainly that was illegal in the South), illegal sex with teenage girls was offered at Glaser's whorehouses, and if Glaser did not have illegal gambling going on in the back rooms of the Sunset Cafe, he certainly did at other locations.

Police raids were so commonplace that they became a joke. Pianist Earl Hines liked to tell the story of how when he heard the police coming, he immediately ran outside to the van so that he would get a good seat. Usually, they were just carted downtown to the police station, booked, and allowed to return to the club. It was not the sort of process that engendered respect for the law, especially since the musicians all knew the cops were on the take and cared no more about the law than they did.

Although Hines and Louis came from starkly different backgrounds—Hines was born in Pennsylvania, where he grew up in a middle-class black family—they shared the same humorous approach to life and the same passion for the music they played. It was said at the time that Hines was as good on the piano as Louis was on the trumpet.

"At critical moments in the course of a solo, Hines's hands would nervously fly across the keyboard, letting loose with a jagged, off-balance phrase, a flurry of notes as agitated as a swarm of honeybees forced from their hive," wrote author Ted Gioia in *The History of Jazz*. "In the midst of this chaos, the tempo of the music would disappear. Time stood suspended."

Working with Louis and Hines at the Sunset Café was the floorshow director, Percy Venable. Aware of the show business aspect of entertaining nightclub crowds, he was always in search of a gimmick, something to attract attention to the bandstand. One of his production gimmicks was built around a song he had written titled "Big Butter and Egg Man." The phrase was a reference to the commonly held belief that the men who went door to door selling eggs and butter often received more than tips from the ladies of the houses they visited.

To highlight the song, Venable paired Louis with a young singer named May Alix. The idea was for them to sing to each other, all the while bringing out the comedy of the song. Louis had trouble with the song, according to Hines, because he was attracted to the singer, and the result was a lot of false starts and miscues that became comedic in themselves. Louis liked the song so much that he composed a monologue that he used midway through the number. It wasn't the type of song that would interest a jazz purist, but it always put a big smile on Louis's face.

In August 1926, Lil purchased a second home, a lakefront summer cottage located in Idelwild, Michigan. She saw the cottage as a good investment, but there was more to it than that. Knowing how much Louis liked to swim, she used it to lure him away from Alpha for a romantic three-week vacation.

There at the cottage, it was just the two of them. Lil was concerned about the negative influence that Glaser, Alpha, and all the hangers-on at the Sunset Café were having on Louis. He was turning into someone she no longer recognized.

The more she gave to Louis, especially in the form of success with the Hot Fives, the more he turned it around on her and used it against their relationship. It is hard to know what was going through Louis's mind during this time (his later writings on this subject often seem self-indulgent), but the reality of it was that he was taking from Lil and giving to Alpha. That was, in fact, a major difference between the women: Lil gave all she had to Louis, and Alpha took all he had—and without apparent remorse.

Lil would later look back on these three weeks as one of the best times of her life. It was the only time, actually, that she ever had her husband entirely to herself, without the distractions offered by her mother, Clarence, and the other musicians who had a habit of intruding unannounced into their home.

Louis also enjoyed himself during the vacation. There were few things he liked better than swimming and he was in the lake every day, often swimming the one-mile distance across the lake and back again. Lil did not like to swim. She tried it once with

Louis in Lake Michigan, but he dunked her and it frightened her so badly that she got out of the water and never re-entered it.

At the cottage, she was content to watch Louis have a good time. She cooked for him, made love to him, talked to him about all the great things she saw for his career, and listened to the plaintive call of his horn at sunset as he serenaded the lake. She did everything she could to woo him back, but when the three weeks were up and they returned to Chicago, he went straight back into Alpha's arms and the wickedness that surrounded the Sunset Café. Lil was losing the war and she knew it, but she was not ready to give up on him yet, not when there were other battles to fight and hopefully win.

On November 16, 1926, Lil and Louis returned to the Okeh Records studio for another session. Lil took two songs she wrote to the session, "Jazz Lips" and "Skid-Dat-De-Dat." Not to be outdone by his wife, Louis took two songs written by Percy Venable, "Big Butter and Egg Man" and "Sunset Café Stomp." Lil must have been unhappy about the songs that Louis brought from the Sunset Café, for along with the songs came May Alix, the light-skinned black woman he worked with at the club. Was Louis trying to flaunt his new life away from Lil? Certainly she could be forgiven for thinking so.

"Jazz Lips" was a tight, stop-time instrumental that allowed Louis to display his fingering dexterity. As Louis's shadow throughout the song, Kid Ory played a nearly flawless trombone. Lil's other composition, "Skid-Dat-De-Dat," gave Louis another opportunity to toss in a chorus of scatting.

Louis never took credit for inventing the scat, as he should have done, but he encouraged others to trace its origins to "Heebie Jeebies" and "Skid-Dat-De-Dat." Said Louis: "Anyway, it doesn't make any difference one way or the other. It's all jive, no matter where it came from, and it all seem(s) to have a friendly attitude."[15]

"Big Butter and Egg Man" features some brilliant trumpet work by Louis, but Alix's tinny vocals offered more personality than musical merit. The sole purpose of "Sunset Café Stomp" seemed to be to promote the dancers at the café, and it may have been recorded at the suggestion of Glaser and his underworld cronies. Nonetheless, Lil plays a solid piano, and Louis and Dodds do some of their best work, all to a distinct Charleston rhythm. Louis's vocal on this track leaned toward the minstrel. Listening to it, it is easy to visualize him wearing the top hat, frock coat and spectacles he wore while performing it at the Sunset Café.

A little over ten days after this session, they returned to record another two songs, "You Made Me Love You" and "Irish Black Bottom." Both were cowritten by Louis and Venable and featured Henry Clark on trombone instead of Ory.

With each record that Okeh released, the fame of Louis and the Hot Fives grew. As the "top gun" on trumpet in Chicago, Louis came under constant assault from wannabes who asked to sit in with the band in an effort to outplay Louis. They never did, of course, for no matter how good they were Louis always was able to reach deep down inside and come up with phrasing or intensity that no one could top.

One night his old friend King Oliver came into the Sunset Café with sheet music for a new song and dared Louis and the other trumpet player to sight-read it there in front of everyone. They took on the dare and performed brilliantly until they hit the break, at which point they fell apart. Without waiting for an explanation, Oliver made a beeline for the door, telling them over his shoulder to let him know when they had learned it.

Louis was disgusted with himself for flubbing the piece and immediately took the other trumpet player to the kitchen to learn the break. At the next intermission, they sent for Oliver. He sat and listened as they played the piece flawlessly. Then he got up to leave, never commenting on the song, until he was on his way out the door. "At last, you've made it," he muttered.

Oliver was not the only music legend dropping in on Louis. In May 1927, jazz pianist and songwriter Fats Waller traveled to Chicago with his seventeen-year-old wife Anita and their infant son, Maurice, to accept a job playing in the pit band at the Vendrome Theatre, where Louis worked on a regular basis.[16]

Lil graciously invited them to stay with her and Louis at their house. The visit went smoothly enough—after they performed at the Vendrome, Waller frequently went with Louis to the Sunset Café, where he sat in with the band. But it all came to a screeching halt one day when a police officer showed up at Lil's house with a warrant for Waller's arrest on charges that he was in arrears in his alimony payments to a former wife. Waller was dragged back to New York to stand trial, leaving his distraught wife and their baby stranded at Lil's house. Not until Anita's mother showed up to rescue her daughter and grandson did life return to normal in the Armstrong household.

During the second and third week of May 1927, Lil and Louis returned to the Okeh studios. Lil took no original songs to those sessions, but Louis arrived with four, "Wild Man Blues," "Potato Head Blues," "S.O.L. Blues," and "Gully Low Blues."

It was at this point that the Hot Fives became the Hot Sevens. The new lineup consisted of Lil on piano, Louis on trumpet, John Thomas on trombone, Johnny Dodds on clarinet, Johnny St. Cyr on banjo, Pete Briggs on tuba, and Baby Dodds on drums. The reason they were able to expand the band to include bass (tuba) and drums was because of new advances in the technology of recording equipment. Okeh had switched over to a new electrical system that allowed them to dump the old megaphone and wax equipment. For the first time, record buyers heard music at a quality much closer to what they would experience hearing it live.

As always, they rehearsed together before going to the studio. "[Louis] would tell each of us when to take a solo or when not to, and who would come in at different times," says Baby Dodds. "We weren't a bunch of fellows to write down anything. That would have made it too mechanical. We would stop and talk it out more than anything else. If there was any writing involved, Lil would write down what the musicians were supposed to do. Of course, we all had our ideas to give the band, and we would work them out at rehearsal."[17]

As if to emphasis the band's newfound freedom of expression, "Willie the Weeper" begins with Baby's cymbal strokes and soon adds Briggs's tuba. The song exploded with a delicious mixture of sounds as Louis displayed tones that had only been hinted at on the earlier tinny recordings and Lil ran up and down the piano keys, relishing the highs and lows and everything in between.

On "Potato Head Blues" Louis played one of the most brilliant solos of his career. It came after he swapped solos with Dodds on clarinet. Mixing low and high notes, he did things on the trumpet that no one had ever before done. Even today it stands as one of the great solos of the twentieth century.

With "S.O.L. Blues," Louis sought to slide a song past his white fans while giving his black admirers a sly wink—S.O.L. is abbreviated slang for Shit Outta Luck. But when executives at Okeh heard it, they shelved the song and kept it off the market for thirteen years. Not willing to waste a song, the band returned to the studio the next day and recorded "Gully Low Blues," a song with an identical arrangement and similar solos. The second version was slightly faster but just as compelling, primarily because of Louis's innovative trumpet work and Dodds's unstoppable clarinet.

"That's When I'll Come Back to You," written by Briggs, pitted poignant vocals by Lil and Louis, with Lil singing the role of a jilted lover and Louis answering that he'll come back when it's "ninety below." Everyone knew about Lil and Louis's marital problems, so it appears that Biggs, the newcomer to the group, was having some fun with them at their expense—and with their approval. Musically, the highlight of the song was the way Dodds tunneled beneath their vocals with his clarinet.

Other songs from those sessions included "Alligator Crawl," "Melancholy," "Weary Blues," "Twelfth Street Rag," and "Keyhole Blues." The two most notable things to emerge from the sessions were the increased emphasis on Louis's vocals and the decreased reliance on Lil's piano. The latter was probably to be expected since Baby's drums supplanted much of the rhythm responsibilities previously carried by Lil.

The thinking of the day had it that the clarinet replaced the upper end of the keyboard and the banjo took the place of the middle ground. The addition of a tuba took the bass note responsibility away from Lil, and the combined efforts of the drums and the banjo displaced the rhythm functions of her piano.

That must have been painful for Lil to accept, though she did so without apparent rancor at the sessions. It is not known whether she had discussions with Louis about it. Lil had organized the group, rehearsed it, provided songs for it, and performed faithfully at every session. Now she was losing the Hot Fives and the Hot Sevens, just as certainly as she was losing the love of her life.

If 1927 was a banner year for American music, it was a heartbreaking one for both Lil and Louis on a personal level. Dempsey was in poor health because of a stroke, and Mayann died that year, apparently of a stroke. Strokes and heart disease resulting from high blood pressure and arterial disease are high among African Americans today, but they were even more of a killer in the early twentieth century when preventative measures were not yet well understood.

Other than a deep love for each other, the one thing that Lil and Louis had in common was a strong emotional attachment to their mothers. When Mayann became ill in New Orleans, Louis had her returned to Chicago so that he could oversee her care. "I did everything in my power to save Mayann," says Louis. "I gave her the finest doctors, and the whole time she was in the hospital it cost me over seventeen dollars a day. I didn't care what it cost, as long as I could save Mayann."[18]

Louis stayed at his mother's side during her final days and Lil comforted Louis the best she could, for Louis was attempting to sever his emotional ties with her even as death was severing his ties with his mother. Lil had never cared for Mayann, feeling that she was too coarse, too ragged about the edges, to ever fit into her own concept of a proper family life. Nonetheless, she understood, perhaps better than anyone else, Louis's bond with his mother, and she assured him that she would still be there for him, no matter what happened in the hospital.

"Son, carry on," Mayann told Louis just before she died at the age of forty-one. "[You] treat everybody right, and everybody white and colored loves you. You have a good heart. You can't miss."[19]

Louis held up well during the funeral services in the hospital chapel, but when the undertaker began to pull the cover back over the coffin, Louis fell apart. "I let out plenty of tears, and I just couldn't stop crying," says Louis. "Mayann was laying there looking so natural, just as though she was just taking a nap."

Mayann's death was just as hard on Lil, and not just because of the compassion she felt for Louis but because of her own fears about Dempsey's mortality. Dempsey and Mayann could not have been more different, yet what they had in common was an historical link to slavery. Lil and Louis were among the first generation of blacks in America to emerge from its shadow. Everything that Dempsey and Mayann did for their children was influenced by the memory of the evils of slavery. What white sons and daughters of America could ever really understand the power of maternal bonds formed under such circumstances?

If Lil pushed herself and Louis beyond normal expectations for black couples of that era, it was because she felt the hopes and dreams of an entire generation that was desperate for a new vision of the future. If they failed, then their mothers failed, too—and Lil was not about to allow that to happen.

On September 2 and 6, 1927, Lil and Louis returned to the Okeh studio, only this time they did so with the Hot Fives—Johnny Dodds on clarinet, Johnny St. Cyr on banjo, and Kid Ory on trombone. Ory had been out of the road with King Oliver during the Hot Sevens sessions, and everyone was glad to see him—and his silky slide work—back in the groove with the band.

No one ever adequately explained why the Hot Fives replaced the Hot Sevens, but the answer clearly lay with Lil, whose music had been pushed aside by the Hot Sevens. There are no words to adequately describe the lifelong intensity of Lil's determination, especially if she felt slighted in any way. As good as they were, the Hot Sevens were now history.

Lil and Louis took no original songs of their own to these two-day sessions, but with Ory back they were eager to hear how the original group would sound on the new electronic equipment. They began the session with "Put 'Em Down Blues," on which Ory and St. Cyr shared opening breaks. During her break, Lil was in fine form as she allowed her right hand to tickle the keys with more abandon than usual. Louis's vocal on this song showed that he had been experimenting with his voice's ability to hit higher notes.

When Okeh executives heard "Ory's Creole Trombone," a song composed by the trombonist several years earlier, they decided to shelve it. Normally flawless, Ory sounds clunky on the song, more like a trombonist in a marching band. To replace it, the band returned four days later with "The Last Time," a song that gave Ory an opportunity to redeem himself with a solo that introduced and effectively played off Louis's vocal.

With Mayann now gone, Louis seemed to gravitate more to Lil than to Alpha, though she and her mother were still very much a part of his life. Louis was beginning to learn that being around incessantly agreeable people had its drawbacks, especially when he needed good advice and received only passive agreement. Louis needed someone other than Lil to tell him to sever his association with the Sunset Café, but Alpha and her mother were enjoying the bounty of that association much too much to want to see it changed.

By 1927, Al Capone's relationship with club owner Joe Glaser had intensified. But there was a downside to hanging out with Capone. With the gang wars in full swing by 1927, any nightclub that Capone visited was a potential target for retribution by his machine gun–toting enemies.

On occasion Capone and his friends showed up and asked for the club to be closed so that they could have a private party. Since Louis enjoyed Capone's company, it did not bother him to play a private party, especially since the mobster and his cronies were generous with their tips, usually issued in the form of one hundred dollar bills.

All that came to an end in November 1927, when Louis's engagement at the Sunset Café ended. That meant he was effectively out of work, though no one expected him to be unemployed for long. As usual, he went to Lil and cried on her shoulder. Despite their marital problems, she was still the closest thing he had to a manager.

Lil responded to Louis's needs by setting up a three-day recording session with Okeh for the Hot Fives, beginning on December 9, 1927, and ending on December 13. This time Lil wrote four of the six songs they rehearsed and took to the session. Louis needed her and she reached deep down inside herself to find songs that would make him money. The result represented some of her very best work.

The first song they recorded, "Struttin' With Some Barbecue," was Lil's masterpiece. For decades, it stood as a measuring rod against which other jazz instrumentals were compared. The hallmark of the song was the way it was allowed to build to the point where Louis played his solo, then tapered off, under Louis's exquisite breath control, to the point where it could dissolve into a gentle, stop-time conclusion. When all was said and done, it was the melody that lingered.

In later years, Louis often took credit for the song's title. After a dance one night, he explained, he and Zutty Singleton drove out to a barbecue joint on Forty-Eighth and State Streets where an old man made some of the most delicious barbecue that "anyone would love to smack their chops on." The problem with eating there was that one order was not enough. He and Zutty ended up going back for seconds. It was at that point that he decided to someday call a song "Struttin' With Some Barbecue."

Louis undoubtedly told Lil about the barbecue while they were sitting on the back steps of their house, where they always worked on songs. It is doubtful that Lil wrote such a melody-driven song to mesh with Louis's song title. Mostly likely the song came first and the title arrived while they were talking about food on the back steps.

Lil and Louis cowrote "I'm Not Rough" for the Okeh session. More blues than jazz, it begins with Lil on the piano and soon moves into two choruses of full instrumentation. Featured in this cut was blues guitarist Lonnie Johnson, who was asked to sit in on the session. After a solo, Johnson plays stop-time guitar beneath Louis's vocal. It's a pretty effective song until the end, when the band speeds up into double time and undercuts Louis's trumpet solo.

The other two songs written for the session by Lil were "Got No Blues," a cheerful romp that tests Louis's impeccable sense of timing, and "Hotter Than That," a song that has similar chord structure to Ory's "Savoy Blues," which they also recorded at this session. The highlights of "Hotter Than That" were Lil's piano work beneath Ory's trombone solo and Louis's scatting, regarded by some as one of his greatest efforts.

"Once In a While," the only other song beside "Savoy Blues" not written by Lil, was a vaudeville-type song that Louis transformed with his energetic phrasing. It was helped along with Ory's relentless trombone and Dodd's bouncy clarinet. Throughout it all, St. Cyr and Lil drove the rhythm along with a steadiness that provided a sturdy platform for the soloists.

When the Hot Fives shut the door on that session, they wrapped up a series of recordings that over the past two years had reshaped American music, though the founding members of the group didn't know it at the time, any more than they knew that they had just recorded their last songs together as a group.

Lil pursued her degree in music from the Chicago College of Music throughout 1928. She never discussed her reasons for doing so, but the fact that Doc Charles Cooke, the musical director of the competing Dreamland (there were two Dreamlands in Chicago—Dreamland Café, where Lil worked, and the Dreamland

Ballroom), had a doctorate from the Chicago College of Music probably played a role in her decision.

It was common practice among racist whites of that era to label blacks that had an education as "Doc" or "Professor." Doc Cooke was a real doctor, the result of his degree, and the most prominent African American to graduate from the school. One of the most prominent white students was David Rose, who was a contemporary of Lil's at the school. He went on to achieve fame as a composer and orchestra leader, his most famous composition being "The Stripper."

Lil's main goal in life had never been to be a working musician. When it came to music, she perceived herself to be an intellectual, someone who broke music down into its component parts and studied it the way pathologists studied the human body. The title of Professor or Doctor fit nicely into the concept of self she had nurtured since childhood. Her relationship with Louis had many facets, but it was her role as teacher that gave her the most satisfaction. Not surprisingly, it was the role that Louis found easiest to accept.

The one constant in their marriage had been Louis's habit of turning to her whenever he got into trouble or needed advice. That was the case early in 1928 when he went to her for help in opening a nightclub of his own. After losing his steady job at the Sunset Café, Louis told his friend, drummer Zutty Singleton, that he was thinking about forming his own band to tour the South. Zutty told him they should stick together, so that anyone who wanted to hire one would have to hire the other. That sounded good to Louis, who then decided to bring Earl Hines into the pact.

The more the "Three Musketeers" discussed their prospects, the more ambitious they became. Hines went a step further and suggested they open their own nightclub, where they would make all the money and not have whites on their case all the time about their music. Louis and Zutty agreed.

"Help!" Louis said to Lil.

Together they went shopping for a location for the club. Louis didn't know anything about leasing or purchasing property. He didn't know anything about permits or licenses. Louis didn't know much about anything except blowing his horn, but setting up the club became his responsibility when Zutty and Hines voted him group leader. It was a high honor, to be sure, but leadership had its drawbacks. In this case, it meant Louis would have to pay for everything.

After two days of searching, Lil and Louis found a location named Warwick Hall, located off Forrestville Avenue. The lease called for a year's guarantee and monthly rent of three hundred and seventy-five dollars. That was an exorbitant amount to pay for rent, but Louis took it, fully expecting to receive a fast return on his investment. It is odd that Lil would allow him to sign a lease involving that much money, but she may have done it to teach him a lesson.

Now that they had their own nightclub, Louis, Hines, and Zutty organized a band to play in the club. They called it the Hot Six. Added to the group were Fred Robinson on trombone, Jimmy Strong on clarinet and tenor saxophone, and Mancy Carr on banjo.

Opening night at the Warwick was a disaster. They had decided against spending money on promotion or publicity, figuring that their fans would hear about the club and be there to show support for the group. Few people came to the club, and those that did demonstrated little or no interest in the music. The band played until it was exhausted, giving the customers the best stuff it had. No one cared.

Unfortunately, a larger, more opulent nightclub called the Savoy Ballroom opened on the same night only a short distance away. It had an electronic billboard and peacocks, the type of glitzy glamour that the Warwick could not give its customers.

Louis again sought Lil's advice, but she didn't know what to tell him. There was no way he could outdo the Savoy. She was glad she had not invested her own money in the club. After weeks of earning about one dollar each per night, the Three Musketeers decided to shut down the club before Louis lost any more of his money.

On the night they closed the doors, the three men trudged over to Louis's car only to discover it had been stolen. They found the car the next day, but not before it had been stripped of all its valuable parts.

Thus began one of the most miserable periods in Louis's life. He couldn't find work anywhere. It was like someone had put out the word on him (maybe they had). The Greatest Trumpet Player in the World was on the skids. Alpha's paycheck for baby-sitting and maid service was the only money coming into the household.

By contrast, Lil was soaring. By day she worked on her degree at the Chicago College of Music and by night she performed in her new band, featuring Louis's old rival Freddie Keppard on trumpet. She described him as a "man about town" who drank to excess and never lacked for female company.

"Personally, I think he was better than King Oliver [on trumpet]," says Lil. "I think he had a better tone. I liked him better."[20] Sometimes they performed on the road in Indiana and downstate Illinois. By all accounts, it was a very successful band.

At the end of June 1928, desperate for both money and recognition, Louis decided to record again with the Hot Fives, only they would be that in name only. For this session he wanted to work with the Hot Sixes. He owed them that much. The only problem was what to do about Lil. She would have to be replaced on piano with Hines.

To Louis's surprise (and great relief), Lil did not react in a hostile way to being dumped from the band. She took the news with good grace, asking only that she be allowed to act as manager for both Louis and Hines. That was fine with them. They then countered her request with one of their own. Would she write a song for the upcoming session? No problem, Lil told them.

When they showed up at the Okeh studio it was with four songs. "Fireworks," the first one they recorded, began with quiet percussion in stop-time and then exploded into a battle of trumpet, cornet, and trombone. Hines's solo stops the movement of the piece cold with altered tempo and inventive licks with his right hand. Each instrument takes a solo, with Louis's providing the rawest energy (as you would expect).

"Skip the Gutter" offers Louis and Hines an opportunity to play dueling solos. There is never much doubt about who the winner will be, but the exercise itself seems to inspire each man to new heights. Clearly, Hines has replaced Johnny Dodds as Louis's main foil. Whereas he used to play to the clarinet, he now played to the piano.

"A Monday Date," a composition that Hines brought to the session, begins with Louis and Hines discussing the song they are going to play, with Louis also mentioning a Chicago concoction named Mrs. Searcy's gin. Louis does a little bit of scatting on the song, but most of his vocal seems patterned after the "crooner" records that were then the rage. His trumpet work is unusual because he uses a mute (a rarity for him) and because he experiments with time changes within his solo.

Lil's song, "Don't Jive Me," was the last song recorded at the session. Her music at this point was becoming more dramatic, especially during the introductions, and this song reflected her growing sense of ensemble instrumentation as a creative counterpoint to the solos. It also contained a strong melody, a distinction that set her apart from other jazz writers of the era. She didn't "feel" music so much as she heard it.

The new Hot Sixes continued recording that year, though without Lil's input, unless, of course, they got into trouble, in which case they would go running to her for help. One example of that occurred when they recorded "West End Blues," a song that later became one of Louis's classics.

Trouble arose when rumors started circulating that Louis had stolen the opening cadenza from King Oliver. Lil jumped into the fray with the explanation that *she* had taught the cadenza to Louis. That made sense, because as many records as Oliver had made, he had never played anything remotely like it.

The incident is interesting not so much because of the dispute itself as for the insight it provides into Lil's working relationship with Louis. He had always said that they worked out their songs sitting on her back steps and not sitting at the piano. Since Lil played no other instrument, that means that she sang her melodies and horn parts to Louis, who then translated his part, on the spot, to what he would play in the studio. It may never be known for certain, but there is a possibility that Louis developed his scatting abilities by imitating her attempts to sing like a musical instrument.

For the remainder of 1928, Lil took her responsibilities seriously as a manager to Louis and Hines. She went to the very club that had put Louis's nightclub out of business, the Savoy Ballroom, and she booked Louis and Hines there with Carroll Dickerson's orchestra.

Then she got him a one-hundred-dollar-a-night booking on the riverboat, the *St. Paul,* which traveled to St. Louis. It must have brought back fond memories to Louis, at least for a while, but before long, his best gig turned out to be his worst nightmare.

One evening so many customers packed on the boat that it nearly sank. Louis returned to Chicago, determined to never

again step foot on a riverboat. The Savoy Ballroom was so happy
to see him back that it raised his salary to an astonishing two hundred dollars a week.

The good times did not last forever at the Savoy Ballroom.
Early in 1929, business started tapering off. More and more
frequently, the club owner went to the band members and asked
them to "carry" him on their paychecks. Delayed payment to a
jazz musician usually meant no payment at all, so Louis and the
others were understandably concerned about their future at the
club. They all had bills to pay and girlfriends and wives to support.

The Chicago economy was already in a downward spiral,
affecting the way people spent their leisure time, but the hardest
blow to the nightclub scene occurred in February with Al
Capone's St. Valentine's Day massacre. It marked the end of the
city's fast times and the beginning of a tough federal crackdown
on organized crime. Since there were few clubs in Chicago not
under the control of organized crime, that meant they became the
first casualties of the nation's war against crime.

Since the bigger picture of what was happening in Chicago
was not immediately apparent, Louis may have blamed his problems on Lil's management. When former Okeh Records executive
Tommy Rockwell, who was based in New York where he worked
as a promoter, sent for him to make some more records, Louis was
happy to have an excuse to leave town. Okeh had turned Louis's
contract over to Rockwell, perhaps with an understanding that he
would continue to make recordings for the company.

Of course, more than making records was involved. Rockwell
wanted to be Louis's manager. Unhappy with Lil's "management"—
and deflated by Alpha's constant requests for money—Louis
dumped both women and went to New York. Rockwell booked

him at a Harlem nightclub named Connie's Inn, where one of the club's silent partners, Dutch Schultz, took an instant liking to the jazzman. Louis didn't know it at the time, but Schultz was one of New York's most feared gangsters.

Not far behind Louis was Lil, who went to New York to study at the New York College of Music (she had received her degree from the Chicago College of Music in 1928). In May she had performed a recital at Carter's Temple CME Church, where she was accompanied at the second piano by her teacher, composer Louis Saar.

Among the music she performed were DeBussy's "Ministrels," three Chopin numbers, and "Serenade Neapolitana and Minuet." In New York she studied to expand her knowledge of classical European music.

Lil began to feel that she had outgrown nightclub performances. Smoky rooms, obnoxious drunks, nightclub brawls—all had seemed more exciting and adventuresome in her early years. Now she wanted more substance out of life.

Lil and Louis were both in New York on October 29, 1929, when the New York Stock Exchange crashed and sent the American economy spiraling out of control. The world would change drastically for musicians, as it would for everyone, but that was not so apparent in the beginning because the demand for performers remained high.

The Jazz Age Throws in the Towel

As the Jazz Age ground to a halt in 1930, thousands of banks across the country closed their doors and tens of thousands of businesses shut down as the Great Depression rolled across the nation. Among the casualties were Prohibition, the speakeasies and nightclubs that were supported by illegal liquor sales, and the musicians and blues singers who thrived in that atmosphere. Hardest hit were African Americans, who found little reason for hope. Harlem, the once-thriving pearl of black culture, descended into despair, ultimately becoming a stark ghetto of broken dreams.

America needed music more than ever, but not the type associated with pain and suffering and not the type associated with gin mills and organized crime. America needed to laugh. It needed a happy, smiling face that would engender memories of better times and hope for the future. If there was ever a person who was in the right place at the right time, it was Louis Armstrong, who, with his expansive smile and soothing voice, seemed the perfect antidote for the troubled times.

Under the guidance of Tommy Rockwell, Louis's career surged, even as the careers of his friends and competitors fell to the wayside. Rockwell affiliated him with a new record label, Victor, and ingratiated him with New York nightclubs owned by the mob, which guaranteed him a steady income while he was in the city.

Like Louis, Lil was a survivor. After obtaining a postgraduate degree from the New York College of Music, she returned to Chicago, where she resumed her career as a bandleader. There was still a market for the sophisticated type of orchestra music she enjoyed performing, and just as she had led the Jazz Age into being she helped lead the way into the fledgling swing era.

Lil was not happy about Rockwell taking over the management of Louis's career. Her motive for managing his career was love, not financial considerations. Louis had an attraction to the dark side of life, and Lil had always seen it as her responsibility to keep him focused on what she considered the bright side. It required lots of love to do that, for it meant criticizing him when he was wrong, and she didn't see how Rockwell could substitute love of money for the type of passionate but practical love she felt for Louis the man.

When she learned in May 1930 that Louis had taken a train from New York to Los Angeles to investigate the music scene there, she put her career on hold and took the next train out of Chicago. That was so unlike Louis to travel by himself. There had to be something wrong with the man for him to do something like that.

What she found when she arrived in Los Angeles was not at all what she had expected. He was doing quite well, actually. After arriving in Los Angeles, he had checked into the Dunbar Hotel, which had a national reputation as a watering hole for blacks in show business.

With nothing arranged with any of the clubs before his arrival, he had no prospects, only a belief that he would find work somewhere. It was while he was getting a haircut in the hotel barbershop that he was recognized by a fan who had connections with several nightclubs. As a result of that chance meeting, Louis was introduced to Frank Sebastian, who owned the Cotton Club in Culver City. Sebastian hired Louis on the spot to front the house band led by Leon Elkins. He even changed the name of the band to "Louis Armstrong and His New Cotton Club Orchestra."

What Lil found when she arrived was a man on top of his game, a man who had landed an important job without the help of Tommy Rockwell or herself. Although probably disappointed that he did not need her, she probably felt a secret pride that he had gone about it the way she had taught him. Throughout the early days of their marriage, he had shown no ambition. Fearful of failure, he always aimed for the lowest level of success. Now he had enough confidence to begin at the top.

One of the benefits of performing at the Cotton Club was the added exposure of the radio broadcasts that emanated from the club each night at eleven o'clock. Lil stayed with Louis in his room at the Dunbar Hotel, but neither of them felt comfortable with her accompanying him to the club each night. Located next to the MGM lot, it was a posh establishment frequented by the top Hollywood stars of that time. Bing Crosby was a frequent visitor, as was filmmaker D. W. Griffith.

Instead of going to the club, she listened to the show in her hotel room. "One night they were playing 'Tiger Rag,'" says Lil. "At the end he makes a high note, but this time he just kept going and going—and he hit it an octave higher than it was supposed to be. I couldn't believe my ears."[1]

When he returned to the hotel, she asked him about the high note.

"The fellows told me I made something different."

"Yes, you made something different," she said, her voice laced with friendly sarcasm.

Lil tried hard to reestablish their relationship, but Louis just seemed to have other things on his mind. By this point, he saw Lil not so much as a soulmate but as someone who could do things for him, much the same way Alpha saw him. He had never really been faithful to Lil and because they never discussed it, he assumed she did not know about his infidelities.

"[I] don't know when or how long Louis had an affair with Alpha," she said to one interviewer. "I can assure you she was not the only one, so I didn't worry too much about it."[2]

Lil's reunion with Louis in Los Angeles got complicated with the arrival of Alpha, who left for the West Coast when she learned that Lil had preceded her there. But Alpha wasn't looking for a confrontation with Lil. Instead of going straight to the hotel from the train station, she went to Louis's dressing room at the Cotton Club. She told him she had gotten a job as a chorus girl in a Chicago nightclub.

By all accounts, Louis was delighted to see her. He set her up in another hotel and continued to see her while he was living with Lil at the Dunbar Hotel.

As the weeks went by, Lil saw less and less of Louis. He stopped returning to the hotel after his performances. She knew what that meant. She may or may not have known about Alpha, but she certainly knew he was involved with another woman. When asked about his absences, she blamed it on his "popularity." Finally, she grew tired of playing the role of the abused wife and told Louis she was ready to return to Chicago. He didn't try to talk her out of it. Instead, he hired a car to drive her back, a departure that left him free to live with Alpha.

With Lil out of the way, Louis more freely indulged his addiction to marijuana. One night during a break at the Cotton Club,

Louis and the drummer went out into the parking lot to smoke a joint. To Louis's horror, two police detectives stepped from behind a car and arrested them for possession of an illegal substance. On the way to the police station, one of the officers told Louis that he listened to his show every night and was a big fan. In that case, Louis told him, he hoped he would not bust him in the chops.

Louis spent nine days in jail before receiving a court date. When he walked into the courtroom, it was filled with reporters, fans, and people claiming to be his manager. One of those present, a tough-looking white man named Johnny Collins, told Louis that he had been sent by Tommy Rockwell. He explained that he was a "fixer," not a lawyer, and he assured Louis that he had nothing to worry about. That turned out to be the case. To everyone's surprise, the judge gave him a suspended sentence and sent him home.

As his fee for "fixing" the court proceeding, Collins demanded a manager's percentage from Louis's paycheck. Louis agreed to pay it and acquiesced in Collins's takeover of his career. Not until his new manager started hiring and firing the members of his band did Louis understand he was in trouble.

When his employment at the Cotton Club ended, Louis gave Collins the slip in March 1931, and he ran home to the only "mama" he had left in his female arsenal.

Lil was not surprised to find Louis on her doorstep. He had wired her from Los Angeles and asked if he could stay at her place. By that time, Lil knew the marriage was over, but she was too depressed to talk to him about it. She gave Louis the run of her house, and she went out to visit friends. In her absence, Louis helped himself to what was in the kitchen and spent the evening listening to her records.

Lil also must have been embarrassed about Louis's arrest. The details had been plastered in the newspapers, and it was the talk of the town. Louis could not leave the house without people shouting, "I thought you were in jail!"

Lil had fought her entire life to overcome the stereotypes associated with being an African American, yet Louis did not seem to care how his actions reflected on himself or his wife or blacks as a whole. He seemed driven by pleasure (his own) and nothing else. For years she had treated him as a child, scolding him for his mistakes and then forgiving him when he promised not to do it again. She knew a losing battle when she saw one.

Johnny Collins followed Louis to Chicago and resumed his managerial duties, booking him at the Regal Theater. Louis put together another band and moved out of Lil's house. This time, she made no effort to keep him there. She was reconciled to the fact that they had a marriage in name only. She still loved Louis with all her heart, but even that no longer seemed enough. What she had run out of was the glue that had held them together for so long—forgiveness.

Lil never spoke publicly about her feelings about Johnny Collins, but she must have said plenty to Louis. Collins looked like a street thug, and she would have seen through him at their first meeting. Although not a virtuoso on the piano, Lil was a successful bandleader and songwriter, and she found that success without the help of marijuana or the criminal underworld. Why couldn't Louis understand that he could have the life he wanted without selling his soul?

After Louis's engagement at the Regal Theater ended, Collins booked him at the Showboat, a popular white nightclub located on Chicago's Loop. Louis put together a band consisting of Charlie Alexander on piano, Zilner Randolph on trumpet, George James on alto sax, Al Washington on tenor sax, Preston Lindsey on bass, and Mike McKendricks on banjo.

Reaction to Louis and his band was enthusiastic; the first night they played overtime, not quitting until just before dawn. For the first time, Louis's white audiences started calling him "Louie," a term of endearment that stuck with him for the remainder of his career. The engagement seemed to promise even better things to come, then trouble struck. Unknown to Louis, Collins and Rockwell were feuding over Louis's contract. That became apparent to Louis when a carload of gangsters appeared at the Showboat and started a fight with patrons in front of the bandstand.

It was a brutal fight. Louis later said he had never seen blacks fight so dirty; at one point a woman was struck over the head with a chair, splintering it into pieces, some of which struck Louis's trumpet. Most of the band members ducked for cover—all except Louis who leaned against a post and continued to play throughout the fight.

Rockwell sent word to Louis that he had booked him at the mob-owned Connie's Inn. Louis turned down the booking, saying that he did not want to return to that particular nightclub. Louis never said so in later years, but it is reasonable that it was Rockwell's mob connections in New York that motivated Louis to take the train to Los Angeles, without telling anyone that he was leaving town.

Louis stood up to Rockwell, but he must have known the matter was not closed. Shortly after the fight at the Showboat, Louis received word on the bandstand that someone was waiting for him in his dressing room. Louis played out the set, then hurried to the dressing room, thinking that it was probably a female admirer or a friend from the old days. It was neither.

Louis was greeted by a "big, burly" white man with a beard. Louis later described him as having a beard "thicker than one of those boys from the House of David," an indication he thought his visitor might have been Jewish.

The man pulled a pistol on Louis and told him that he was going to New York to perform at Connie's Inn. When Louis responded that was news to him, that his manager, Johnny Collins, had told him nothing about a booking at Connie's Inn, the man pointed the pistol at Louis's head and said, "You're leaving tomorrow morning."

"Well, maybe I am going to New York!" Louis conceded.[3]

With the pistol pressed to his side, the man escorted Louis to a phone booth, where he placed a call to New York. Louis recognized the voice on the other end of the line. "When are you gonna open here?" the voice asked.

Louis looked into the face of the man with the gun and answered, "Tomorrow A.M."

Louis never made that trip, perhaps figuring that he would end up dead even if he did honor the booking at Connie's Inn. Instead, he went to Lil and asked for help. This was beyond Lil's problem-solving capabilities. She told him to get him out of town—and fast. To do that, he needed bookings. He turned to Collins, who canceled the remainder of the engagement at the Showboat.

Within hours, he had Louis and the band out on the road, touring the Midwest and Southeast with a series of one-night stands. After weeks of living the hard life on the road, they arrived in New Orleans for a one-nighter. While there, the manager of the Suburban Gardens offered the band a three-month engagement.

Louis thought he might be safe on his old stomping grounds, so he agreed to stay. The only "organized" crime he saw in New Orleans in his youth came from the black gangs that tried to control the streets. He naively thought that the sophisticated type of crime that inhabited New York and Chicago under the leadership of Al Capone and Dutch Schultz had no foothold in New Orleans.

Of course, things had changed in New Orleans since his departure more than a decade ago. New Orleans had its own branch of the New York mob, and if anything it was even more potent that its big city cousin.

Coinciding with Louis's departure from Chicago was a federal crackdown on Al Capone and Dutch Schultz. It had begun with the St. Valentine's Day Massacre. The crime was so bloody, so flagrant, that it embarrassed not only the federal government, but other crime families across the nation, especially in New York.

Capone was summoned to Atlantic City in May 1929 for what turned out to be the largest underworld conference ever known. One result was the formation of a national commission composed of all the crime families represented. They agreed to honor established territories and to abide by a code for resolving conflicts between families. Another result of the gathering was unanimous agreement that Capone would have to tone down his business dealings in Chicago. The St. Valentine's Day Massacre had put heat on all of them.

Not reaching an agreement with Capone was the federal government. The gangster was able to fend off prosecutions for murder, prostitution, and gambling because they were not federal crimes and he had firm control of the Chicago police.

The federal government tried to nab Capone on federal crimes related to Prohibition, but he was much too crafty to be directly linked to his bootlegging operations. Instead, they went after his money, correctly concluding that he had not paid a proper amount of taxes on his illegal income. In 1931, he was convicted of income tax evasion and sentenced to serve an eleven-year sentence in a federal penitentiary.

Also under investigation on the same charges was Dutch Schultz. Spearheading that investigation was U.S. Attorney Thomas E. Dewey, known to be the toughest in the nation. Indicted on tax evasion charges, Schultz stood trial in Syracuse, New York, only to be released after the jury deadlocked at a seven-to-five vote for conviction. Dewey tried him a second time, this time in the small town of Malone, New York. This time Schultz was acquitted by the jury.

Undeterred, Dewey pursued him on racketeering charges that included murder.

In August 1931, once Louis got settled in New Orleans, Lil took the train to visit him. He was, after all, still her husband. What she found when she arrived did not make her happy: Alpha also had joined Louis in New Orleans.

On top of that, she learned that Louis was not as secure in the city as he—and she—had hoped. The local musicians union had expelled his band members because it had received a complaint that Louis had not honored a booking at Connie's Inn in New York. Louis and the band decided to perform anyway. For that, they were called down to the union offices and questioned about the affair.

Then race became an issue as radio advertisements began airing charges that Louis and his band were taking jobs away from white musicians. After that, they noticed that they were followed by four white men every place they went. The turmoil even spilled over into the Suburban Gardens, where Louis's band had the distinction of being the first black group to ever perform in the club.

Blacks were excluded from the club that night, but they gathered outside so they could hear the music through the doors and windows. Others planned to listen to Louis and his band on the radio. There was a microphone in front of the bandstand, and the music was scheduled to be transmitted live on the radio.

As time came for Louis and the band to be introduced, a crisis was precipitated when the white announcer refused to introduce that he called "that nigger man." Louis did not back down. He approached the microphone and did the introductions himself.

Lil did not take comfort in the controversy. What she couldn't understand was why Louis had to do everything the hard way. If only he had listened to her in the first place, he would not now be dodging mobsters and inflaming the passions of white racists. For the life of her, she could not understand why she could live her life without the slightest hint of controversy and Louis could not go a single day without getting in serious trouble with the police and thugs carrying guns.

The next morning after arriving, Lil waited until Alpha left the room, then she entered and confronted Louis about their situation. Things could not continue the way they were going. Louis told her he thought the problem was that she was too old-fashioned for him. Lil did not disagree with that. She was making the same argument, only approaching it from the standpoint of him being too radical for her.

Lil had dreaded this moment for a long time, but she understood what she had to do. "I think it's best if you go your way and I go my way, and we'll remain friends," she said. "He thought I was joking, but I wasn't joking at all."[4]

After the confrontation, Lil went down to the lobby, identified herself as Mrs. Armstrong, and asked for the keys to Louis's car. Then she asked for the "best-looking" bellboy in the hotel and paid him to drive her back to Chicago.

Later, rumors circulated that Lil had threatened Louis with a .38-caliber pistol. When asked about it, Lil laughed: "I never owned, used or carried a gun in my life. I don't know who started that wild lie. I can tell you now that if I had used one, the whole world would have known beyond a doubt. I wouldn't have missed my target. Dig?"[5]

Four weeks after Lil's confrontation with Louis, Johnny Collins decided to lease a bus and put Louis and the band out on the road. The New Orleans engagement had about run its course, and with racial tensions still running high, getting out of town seemed prudent. From September 1931 until February 1932, they did a series of one-nighters, mostly throughout the South.

One of the most interesting stops was in Lil's hometown of Memphis. When they pulled into the city, Collins's wife, who was traveling with the band to coordinate travel arrangements, asked for a new bus, one that had a long, soft seat in the rear for Louis to nap on. Bus company officials came aboard the bus to talk to Collins's wife, but what they saw—Louis sitting on the arm of her seat—so enraged them that they left the bus and called the police. Integration of any kind was illegal in Memphis, as it was across the South. As a result, they were all taken into custody by the police.

The matter was resolved after the theater owner intervened on their behalf, but the police chief insisted that Louis and the band do a live radio broadcast as a condition of their release. Louis agreed to do it and graciously dedicated the broadcast to the police chief. Their first song was "I'll Be Glad When You're Dead, You Rascal, You."

Much to Louis's misgiving, Collins booked them in New York at the Paramount-Publix Theatre on Broadway. Collins assured Louis that they were far enough away from Connie's Inn that they would be able to slip into town and do a performance without being noticed.

That was not the case, however. Before the performance even took place, Louis was served with court papers; Tommy Rockwell had sued him for breach of contract. Louis countersued, but the performance was canceled.

Blocked in their efforts to find work in New York, the band returned to Chicago where it encountered similar difficulties. Restless and unable to work, Louis struck out for Los Angeles, where he hoped to rekindle the success of his previous visit.

When that, too, ended in failure, he and Collins worked out a plan for him to go to Europe, where jazz was beginning to catch on in a big way. On July 9, 1932, Louis, Alpha, Johnny Collins, and his wife sailed for London. Except for a period between November 1932 and July 1933, when he returned to America to attempt another tour, only to face the same problems with the same gangsters, Louis lived in London and Paris, performing all over Europe to enthusiastic crowds.

As the months went by, Louis's relationship with Collins deteriorated. Often drunk, Collins was verbally abusive of Louis, frequently using racial epithets to berate him in front of other people. Finally, Louis had enough of his crude behavior and fired him. He found a French promoter who put together a tour of France, Belgium, and Italy. Midway through the tour, Louis developed problems with his lip and asked the promoter to cancel the remainder of the shows. The promoter responded by filing a lawsuit against Louis. He claimed Louis canceled because he felt overshadowed by the pianist.

With no manager to speak for him—and fearful of a culture and legal system he did not fully understand—Louis panicked and set sail for America in January 1935. He was hopeful that things had changed in America in his absence, but in some ways it had only gotten worse. The Depression was still raging, and organized crime was in the news as much as it was when Louis left the country.

With Capone in prison, the gangster who was attracting the most attention was Louis's nemesis, Dutch Schultz. U.S. Attorney

Thomas E. Dewey had been shadowing him since 1932, and word was out that he had the goods on Schultz this time.

The gangster responded by putting out a contract on Dewey. Aware of the implications of that, the chosen hitman went directly to Mafia boss Charlie Luciano and informed him of Schultz's plans. The murder of a federal prosecutor was strictly forbidden without the unanimous consent of all members of the crime family commission. Fearful that Schultz was out of control, other New York crime families put out a contract on Schultz. In October 1935, he was dining at a New Jersey restaurant with three associates when gunmen entered and cut them down as they sat at the dinner table.

There must have been times when Louis wondered how he ever got himself in such desperate situations. All he ever wanted to do was make a living blowing his horn. Instead, he spent most of his time scrambling for work, hiding from gangsters, suffering racial insults, and searching for female companionship. Despite his outgoing stage persona, Louis was still very shy around strangers. He had few close friendships, not even among the band members he lived and traveled with for much of the year.

Louis took one look at what awaited him in New York, none of which was encouraging, and he quickly moved on to Chicago to get counsel from the only person who had never let him down.

 "Where's my money?" Lil asked.

Louis was dumbfounded. "What money?"

Lil reminded him that he had promised to send her money. She didn't need to remind him. He had given money to Johnny Collins to forward to Lil. As they talked, he realized that Collins had not sent her the money. He pleaded with her, explaining that it was not his fault.

This time she was in no mood for reconciliation. Louis had been away for three years, living it up in style with Alpha, making no telling how much money, while she struggled to make ends meet.

Louis gave her a familiar litany of troubles: he had no money, the gangsters were after him again, and—this was a new one—he had hurt his lip in Europe and could not play his trumpet. How much of that Lil believed we do not know, but she obviously doubted enough of it to turn Louis away that day and then seek the services of a lawyer.

Louis's homecoming was not what he had expected: he was slapped with a six thousand dollar lawsuit which asked for payment of the money he had promised to send Lil from overseas. At that point in their marriage, Lil did not want to hear any more excuses, even if they were likely to be true. She had told him that associating with gangsters would lead to nothing but trouble. She told him that he was doing the wrong thing by allowing Collins to be his manager. She told him that Alpha was only interested in his money. If she could see all those things, why couldn't he?

After her confrontation with Louis in New Orleans, she had returned to Chicago and begun rebuilding her own music career. Fed up with men, she formed two all-female bands in the latter part of 1931 and 1932. One of the bands, the Harlem Harlicans, featured Leora Mieux, Fletcher Henderson's wife, on trombone and Alma Scott, Hazel Scott's mother, on clarinet and saxophone.

In 1933 she was asked to join an all-male band based in Buffalo, New York. The band backed violist Stuff Smith, but they were having problems and an agent asked them if they would like to leave Smith and team up with Lil.

"Well, the whole band quit Stuff and went with Lil," said George Clarke, who played sax with the band. "But we said, 'We don't know Lil, so we want our own leader.' He would collect the money and pay us all and be in charge of the music, and Lil would just front the band. So he agreed to that. And then when Lil came we went to work in the Vendome Hotel in Buffalo, we all fell in love with Lil, and we were sorry that we had selected our own leader, because we liked Lil so well."[6]

The promoter billed Lil as "Mrs. Louis Armstrong," making certain that the words "Louis Armstrong" were much larger than "Mrs." Additionally, the trumpet player, Jonah Jones, was billed as "King Louis II." The ploy worked, but not entirely the way the promoter had hoped.

Fans weren't fooled into thinking that Louis Armstrong was a member of the band. On the contrary, they assumed that Lil and Jones were Louis's mother and father. Of course, that situation didn't make Lil, who was thirty-five when the band first went out on the road, very happy when she found out about it.

Because they were in the midst of the Depression, the band had a difficult time maintaining enough bookings for everyone to be able to make a living. Band members averaged only five dollars a night; that was not too bad for the times as long as they were able to work seven days a week, but that was seldom the case. The bands that were making top dollar were the big swing orchestras fronted by Duke Ellington, Cab Calloway, and Jimmie Lunceford, who, like Lil, was from Memphis.

For their performances, Lil wore a glamorous white gown and a top hat, and she used a baton to direct the band. Often she did the arrangements for the band. The male musicians admired her work ethic so much that they went out of their way to please her.

In later years, the musicians marveled at how she was able to hold the band together during such tough times. They repaid her confidence in them by always showing up on time and never reporting to the bandstand drunk.

What Lil's band needed most was a job at a hotel where they could get constant exposure and radio airtime. They never got a break like that, primarily because the country was not ready for a female bandleader, and by 1935 they were forced to disband.

"I never could figure that out—and she was so nice, you kinda feel more sorry for her than anything else, 'cause you knew she was trying," says Jones. "See, we knew we had a great band, she knew we had a good band, and then after that, I think she just stopped bothering about it."[7]

Lil returned to Chicago and put together another nightclub and recording band that included Joe Thomas on trumpet, Buster Bailey on clarinet, Teddy Coleman on piano, Huey Long on guitar, Chu Berry on tenor sax, and John Frazier on string bass. She named the new group Lil Hardin Armstrong and Her Swing Orchestra. Now that she had stepped away from the piano, she devoted her time to doing the vocals, arranging the music, and writing the songs.

Chicago had always been her kind of town, at least musically, so she had no problem re-establishing herself on the nightclub scene. The year after returning, she landed a recording deal with Decca Records. On October 27, 1936, Lil Hardin Armstrong and Her Swing Orchestra recorded six songs at Decca's Chicago facilities, five of which were her own compositions.

"Just for a Thrill," the standout song of the session, went on to become, along with "Struttin' With Some Barbecue," one of Lil's most admired and recorded works. More clearly than any other song she wrote, the lyrics of "Just for a Thrill" reflected the tortured love she felt for Louis, a love that vowed to remain true despite being treated as a "plaything" to be tossed around at will. She wrote the song without an instrumental bridge, preferring to allow the trumpet and clarinet to conclude the song with battling solos, with perhaps the trumpet getting the edge with a riff that sounded more like the old Louis than the new version.

"Brown Gal," another of Lil's compositions, is most notable for its combination of stop-time trumpet solos and a splendid tenor sax solo by Chu Berry that was years ahead of its time. Lil's vocal shows tremendous growth since her early attempts with the Hot Fives. She never reaches for notes she can't hit, and the result is entirely convincing. Interestingly, the lyrics reflect one of the differences that set her apart from black male vocalists of that era: Lil was proud of her color, and this song was written as a celebration of that pride. It would be another thirty years before other black artists sang with that much pride.

For "Doin' the Suzie-Q," Lil reached back to the old days for an energetic introduction that had the ensemble blend together until she could break the song into a swing dance number powered by her spirited vocal and another strong tenor sax solo.

"My Hi-De-Ho Man" shows Lil at her mischievous best doing some effective scatting of her own as the lead-in to the trumpet solo. The vocal is flirtatious and plays to the crowd, a quality she considered essential to a successful swing song. Lil's final composition for the session, "It's Murder," was along the same lines, offering both dance music and lyrics that allowed Lil to interact with the audience. She went for humor with this song and her longer-than-usual scat at the end caps it off nicely.

Louis was shocked at Lil's lawsuit. He had always been able to sweet-talk her into anything. This time he was telling the truth. He *had* instructed Johnny Collins to send her money on a regular basis. It wasn't his fault that Collins had not taken care of business. Or was it? That was more or less Lil's point: that it was Louis's fault for choosing the wrong person to handle his money.

But as discouraging as Lil's lawsuit was, it was nothing compared with the other troubles that greeted him upon his arrival in the United States. He was so broke that he was forced to sell his

Buick, which had cost him thirty-two hundred dollars, for a mere three hundred ninety dollars, just to pay his living expenses.

The Depression had forced most of the nightclubs down, but even if that were not the case, he would have had a difficult time finding work because of a lawsuit filed by Johnny Collins, who had obtained a court injunction prohibiting Louis from booking any engagements through any other agent. Add to that the fact that his lip was still hurt and his doctor told him not to play his trumpet for another six months.

Louis was desperate. Except for Alpha, who was nagging him to divorce Lil and marry her—and Lil, who was suing him and refusing to give him a divorce—all of the people who were causing him trouble were white. Most of Louis's Chicago friends had gravitated to other places.

In truth, he didn't have a lot of male friends. He was too much of a loner to ever engage in much male bonding. Most of his male friends had been his employers, like King Oliver (who was then living in New Orleans). His only white friends had been gangsters. The two things that he had always turned to in the past to get him out of trouble—his trumpet and the women in his life—were not options at this point.

Louis recalled the advice he had received before leaving New Orleans: "Be sure and get yourself a white man that will put his hand on your shoulder and say, 'This is my nigger!'" Northern critics, white and black, not familiar with southern culture have always interpreted that as an "Uncle Tom" attitude.

In fact, it is just the opposite. It is based on a southern saying that predates the Civil War: "My nigger can beat your nigger." It is so ingrained in southern culture that it exists to this day, especially in college athletics, where the phrase has the same meaning but is spoken somewhat differently: "Our boys can beat your boys!"

The advice that Louis received was based on the belief that there is nothing lower in life than a white person who has "gone bad." The only way to beat someone like that is to recruit a white person of your own that is even dirtier and low-down. The advice is a cynical realization that you cannot fight bad intentions with pretty music. Louis was fed up with whites, for whom he was beginning to have a minimum regard, and he wanted to give them a taste of their own wicked medicine.

Besieged by problems, Louis turned to one of the dirtiest white men he had ever met, Joe Glaser. He had watched him dance around Capone and his men in the Sunset Café, and they seemed to like the way he did business. He knew about Glaser's scrapes with the law, about his weakness for young girls, about his mobster associations, but none of that mattered. The man fought dirty, and that was exactly what he wanted.

Despite once describing Glaser as a "crude sonofabitch," he went to him, hat in hand, and begged him to be his personal manager. "You needed a white man to get along," he once explained to *Harper's* magazine. "I was tired of being cheated and set upon by scamps and told [him] how my head was jumping from all of that business mess. . . . I told him, 'Pops, I need you. Come be my manager. Please! Take care of all my business and take care of me. Just lemme blow my gig'. . . . Sometimes [he] says I'm nuts. Says it wasn't as bad as as I recall it. But then Papa Joe didn't have to go through it. He was white. Not that I think white people is any naturally meaner than colored. Naw, the white man's just had the upper hand so long—and can't many people handle being top cat."

Louis and Glaser never signed a formal, written contract, so details of their arrangement are scarce. One story has it that Glaser asked for half of Louis's income. Another story has Louis telling that all he wanted out of the deal was one thousand dollars a week, and his expenses and taxes paid—Glaser could keep the rest, no matter how much the total income came to.

Louis's offer arrived at a good time for Glaser. He had recently been indicted on robbery charges, and although he knew the prosecution's case would fall apart because of their inability to find a witness to testify against him, he thought it might be prudent to get out of town for a while.

Glaser wasted no time getting started. First, he made a deal with Johnny Collins, buying him out for five thousand dollars. Then he got busy lining up bookings for Louis, scheduling them so they would not begin until his lip had healed. He told Louis he would have to work out his problems with Alpha himself, but that he would be happy to intervene on his behalf with Lil.

Glaser despised Lil because he knew of her dislike of his lifestyle and because he was aware of the continuing influence she had with Louis. He worked out a way for Louis to resolve his financial disagreement with her, but he frequently told Louis lies about Lil and worked to undermine his faith in her.

The Decca releases were so successful that Lil and the band were asked to relocate in New York in 1937 so that they could record in the facilities there and take advantage of a larger nightclub scene.

On April 15, 1937, Lil and her swing orchestra recorded four new sides for Decca, all cowritten by Lil. Joe Thomas on trumpet and Buster Bailey on clarinet stayed with the band, but the others were replaced with Robert Carroll on tenor sax, James Sherman on piano, Arnold Adams on guitar, Wellman Braud on string bass, and George "Pop" Foster on drums.

The first song, "Born to Swing," shows a band that has moved farther away from the Chicago style of blues-based jazz that had shaped Lil's early years. Instead, the band moves toward the swing grove that was sweeping the nation. In her vocal, Lil keeps the scat, but sings in a more commercially sophisticated style than ever before. The drums are a real asset and provide a good match for Lil's high energy vocal.

"(I'm On A) Sit-Down Strike for Rhythm" starts with a dramatic piano cadence and then breaks into horn-flogging, uptempo swing number that shows Lil again aiming, hopefully, for a commercial audience. Lil slows down the tempo with "Bluer Than Blue," a ballad that features two soulful trumpet solos by Thomas and an uninspired sax solo by Carroll. "I'm Knocking at the Cabin Door," the final song of that session, has an inspired jazz-laced piano solo and some solid trumpet work, but the real value of the song is the insight it offers into Lil's continued yearning for Louis's company at their cottage in Michigan.

On April 15, 1937, they returned to the studio for their second session of the year. There were changes in the band, with Shirley Clay replacing Thomas on trumpet and Prince Robinson replacing Carroll on clarinet. This time Lil cowrote three of the four songs they recorded. Always a prolific songwriter, she was beginning to write with an audience in mind instead of simply expressing her feelings and moods.

"Lindy Hop" is a dance tune, pure and simple, as is "You Mean So Much to Me" (the only song Lil did not write for this session). "When I Went Back Home" has a full-throttle swing engine, but it is filled with Chicago-style jazz riffs, especially on clarinet, which may be why she gave the song the title she did.

Lil does a really nice job with her vocal on "Let's Call It Love," and Bailey's clarinet solo is inspired, probably his best for the entire year. In fact, there is an ear-catching tension between Lil's downward spiraling vocal and Bailey's upstream riff. That being said, the most tantalizing thing about this song is its obvious influence on the Beatles' most debated song, "Sgt. Pepper's Lonely Hearts Club Band."

In between sessions, Lil was walking on the sidewalk in front of the Lafayette Theatre, near the corner of 131st Street and Seventh Avenue, when she ran into a familiar face—Jelly Roll Morton.

"Well, I didn't recognize him at first, and then people said, 'There's Jelly,'" says Lil. "I looked over, you know, and then I walked up to him and introduced myself. I said, 'You know, I heard you play when I was in a music store years ago. You influenced my playing. I heard you play something loud and strong that day and I started playing just like you.'"

Morton looked at her and laughed.

Sensing that he was pleased, she said, "Oh, how you did influence me! And I've been playing loud ever since!"

"I did, did I?" he said. "And did I find you a job?"

Sensing an approaching request for a token of her gratitude, she laughed and said, "No, you didn't find me a job!"[8]

Morton was in need of a job himself. In the late 1920s, he had moved to New York, where he had a high-profile career until Victor Records dropped him from its roster in 1930. Unable to find work, he drifted to Washington, D.C., and tried his hand at promoting fights. When that failed, he lived off his savings until the money ran out. Then he sold the diamonds in his teeth, all but one, that is. He was in New York trying to find work on the day Lil ran into him on the street.

The year after that, Morton was asked to record again by several New York labels, but the renewed interest in his career was short-lived. Again broke and unrecognized for his musical contributions, Morton made his way to Los Angeles, where he died in 1941. No one attended his funeral and the night before he was buried someone broke into the funeral home and stole Morton's last remaining diamond tooth.

Lil ended 1937 with a visit to Memphis, her first since she moved to Chicago. Booked at the Beale Street Palace for one week, she was billed as a "swing queen." After headlining a show at the Palace for blacks each night, she did a second, midnight "ramble" for white Memphians.

On February 2, 1938, she returned to the Decca studios for a new recording session. Her band was totally reconstructed, with Ralph Muzillo and Johnny McGee alternating on trumpet, Al Philburn on trombone, Tony Zimmers on clarinet and tenor sax, Frank Froeba on piano, Dave Barbour on guitar, Haig Stephens on bass, and Sam Weiss on drums. She only brought two songs of her own to the session, perhaps distracted by divorce negotiations that had begun with Louis's lawyer.

The first of Lil's songs, "Let's Get Happy Together," begins with a breathy (and lengthy) trumpet solo and goes into a vocal in which Lil sings about turning to another man after losing her lover. It's a pop song with a swing rhythm and a rolling sax solo that keeps the music on track to a big finish.

Ever transparent in her songwriting, Lil's second song, "Happy Today, Sad Tomorrow," reflects the emotional ups and downs she was experiencing at the time. Her heart is "full of devotion," but she recognizes the dark clouds on the horizon. The muted trumpet and sax interplay during the introduction foreshadow the big-band arrangements that Glenn Miller would make famous in the 1940s.

"Oriental Swing," one of the songs Lil did not write, begins with a drum solo, still a rarity in those days, but it is not enough to save the song, which is easily the least effective she ever recorded. Was Lil sending Louis a message with "You Shall Reap

What You Sow," another song she did not write but felt drawn to? Lyrically, it is a warning to an ex-lover that he will someday regret turning his back on her. Musically, Philburn's trombone and Zimmers's sax provide the song with just the sizzle it needs.

Only weeks after that session, Lil received word that King Oliver had died. After moving to New Orleans, his career had fallen apart. He played one-nighters for a while with pick-up bands, but even that was short lived. Alone and unhappy, he moved to Savannah, Georgia, where he worked as a poolroom janitor and roadside vendor.

While in Savannah in 1937, Louis went shopping for some food. He saw a pushcart peddler and tapped him on the shoulder. When the man turned around, he saw that it was Oliver. The man he had idolized for so many years had become a wretched peddler who lived in poverty. Louis left town devastated by what he had seen.

Oliver tried to make enough money to purchase a train ticket to New York, where his sister lived, but his heart had other plans. He died in his sleep before that happened. Equally poor, his sister used her rent money to bring his body to New York, where he was buried at Woodlawn Cemetery in an unmarked grave.

This was turning out to be Lil's worst year. She had not been close to Oliver in many years, but she respected his work and appreciated Louis's admiration for him. On the heels of the funeral, Glaser pressured her to give Louis a divorce so that he could marry Alpha. If she really cared about Louis, the argument went, she would let him go so that he could find his own happiness. Lil had been holding out on this issue for years, hoping that Louis would find his way back to her, but now she knew that was never going to happen.

Added to that was the difficulty she was experiencing working as a female bandleader. While she never had problems with the male band members, for they almost always loved her, she did encounter stiff resistance from promoters and ballroom managers. Not only was she female, she was black—and that represented two huge obstacles to achieving the level of success she desired.

On September 9, 1938, Lil returned to Decca for another recording session. Her reorganized band was smaller, but packed more punch. There was Reunald Jones on trumpet, a gifted musician who later worked with Count Basie, J. C. Higginbotham on trombone, Lil's old friend Buster Bailey on clarinet, Wellman Braud on bass, and O'Neill on drums. Unlike the previous sessions, Lil both sang and played the piano.

Of the four songs recorded, Lil wrote three. The first of her songs, "Safely Locked Up in My Heart," shows her working out the pain she felt over losing Louis. It is an effective song without knowing Lil's state of mind, but once that is factored in it becomes a moving tribute to lost love. Jones's splendid trumpet solo is reminiscent of Louis in his early years and captures the emotional intensity of the vocal.

With "Everything's Wrong, Ain't Nothing Right," Lil gives us more of the same. It tells the story of a woman whose man has walked out on her. She can't eat, she can't sleep—nothing is working for her. Even the clock in the hallway has stopped. All she can do is mourn and weep. Higginbotham slips into the mood perfectly with a trombone solo that stays within the perimeters set by the vocal.

"Harlem on Saturday Night" and Lil's "Knock-Kneed Sal (On the Mourner's Bench)" are both dance tunes that feature some spirited exchanges among trombone, clarinet, and trumpet, with the latter clearly the winner. Never strong on dance tunes, Lil does precisely what she has to do and then steps back, except on "Knock-Kneed Sal," on which she shares the vocal with Higginbotham.

Three weeks after that session, worn down by the stresses of the year, Lil relented and agreed to give Louis a divorce. "Louis didn't really want to marry Alpha, but she was threatening him with a breach of promise suit, and he was afraid of all the publicity, so he asked me not to give him a divorce, because that would be the only way he could really get out of it," says Lil, explaining her long delay.[9]

Under the terms worked out by her lawyer and Glaser, she charged Louis with desertion, but waived any claim to alimony. On September 30, 1938, the courts finalized the divorce. The most important musical collaboration in American history was at an end.

"My Secret Flame"

There are no sure-fire remedies for a broken heart. As her marriage to Louis was falling apart, Lil threw herself into her music, losing herself in the exotic rhythms and sweet melodies that had been so much a part of their relationship. Once the marriage was over, there seemed less reason to do that.

Lil and Louis never had a child, not the cuddly, burping kind, anyway. Their only offspring was more ephemeral and demanding in its expectations. They never gave it a name, though others called it by its nickname—*jazz*.

Throughout the 1930s, the pain that Lil felt over her troubled relationship with Louis was evident in her music. If she was not trying to woo him back, she was trying to impress him with her own success. Music was the language through which they communicated, whether on her back steps or long distance between cities.

Lil began the 1940s in a deep depression. Lil was one of those rare individuals who fall in love and mate for life, even if the feelings are not mutual with the other partner. There were no second acts in her love life, and she accepted that.

On March 18, 1940, she returned to the studio for what would turn out to be her final session for Decca. This time, except for Wellman Braud on bass, the band was completely revamped. The good news was that her old friend Jonah Jones would play trumpet. The bad news was that all the vocals would be done by Midge Williams and Hilda Rogers. Lil would play piano, with Don Stovall on alto sax, Russell Johns on tenor sax, and Manzie Johnson on drums. Lil brought only one song to the session.

"Sixth Street," a high-energy instrumental, begins with a drum introduction reminiscent of many rock 'n' roll records that would follow fifteen years later. The trumpet, alto sax, and tenor sax play in unison for a while, then Jones breaks out with several strong trumpet solos.

If Lil was not depressed when the session began, she certainly must have been when she heard the playback. With no guitar or banjo, the rhythm section consisted solely of the drums, piano, and bass. On the playback, Lil would have heard only the drums.

A second instrumental, "Riffin the Blues," is a hard-driving swing number that features Lil on piano and Jones on trumpet. Reflecting a new trend in which the solo instrument plays primarily against the drums instead of the other horns and reeds, each player, including Lil, takes turns hitching a ride on the drummer's groove.

The pace slows with a ballad titled "Why Is A Good Man So Hard to Find?" The vocalist, either Williams or Rogers, tries a little too hard, sometimes sending her voice into a nerve-grinding vibrato that the tenor sax attempts to redeem with an underplayed solo. Occasionally, Lil's piano can be heard in the background.

Lil's song, "My Secret Flame," is about unfulfilled love and the pain of watching from a distance. As usual in Lil's songs there is an element of humor; in this case with references to "calling a spade a spade" (sometimes people treated Lil as if they thought she should be ashamed of being black; on the contrary, she was proud of her skin color and celebrated it in many ways, including humor). The vocalist (Williams or Rogers) does a much better job on this one, but the highlight of the song is Jones's muted trumpet solo.

All in all, this was the least impressive of Lil's sessions with Decca. To begin with, her heart wasn't in it; and when she realized she was being phased out of her own band, she didn't think that maintaining her relationship with Decca was worth fighting for. Instead, she packed her bags and went back home to Chicago.

Ten days after receiving his divorce from Lil, Louis married Alpha, although why exactly is not clear since he was already involved with another woman named Polly Jones. When Jones learned he had remarried, she filed a breach-of-promise lawsuit against Louis, claiming that he had promised to marry her once the divorce was finalized.

Louis's love life was in a mess, as usual. Shortly after his marriage to Alpha—and the lawsuit from Polly Jones—he performed at the Cotton Club in New York, where he met a twenty-four-year-old chorus girl named Lucille Wilson. Her skin was darker than most of the women for whom he had fallen, and her figure was full, not her best asset. But there was something about her that intrigued him. Later, he explained his attraction by saying it was because she seemed innocent and uninterested in his money. There is also the fact that, despite her youth, she had a very matronly appearance.

For Louis, it was love at first sight, and he began a secret affair with Lucille that lasted several years. As his love for Lucille increased, his feelings for Alpha decreased—and by all accounts it was mutual. Disappointed in Louis's decreasing ability to provide her with the luxuries she craved, she started seeing other men.

Louis's marital problems became public knowledge in January 1942 when columnist Walter Winchell wrote about their difficulties (of course, the story may have been planted by Glaser, in view of his reported relationship with Winchell).

Louis responded to Winchell with a letter confirming the columnist's allegations that Alpha had taken up with another man. Wrote Louis: "Thank God. If I could only see him [the man Alpha started living with] and tell him how much I appreciate what he's done for me by taking that chick away from me."[1]

This time Louis sued for divorce, charging Alpha with desertion. If Winchell's column was not a plant, a favor done for Glaser, it certainly had the same effect, for it made Alpha's transgressions public knowledge and opened the door to a divorce in which it was unlikely Louis would have to pay alimony.

On October 2, 1942, the divorce was finalized. The marriage had been a nightmare for Louis from the very beginning. "To believe that Alpha turned out in later years to be a no good bitch," he subsequently observed, "why I am still flabbergasted."[2]

Five days after his divorce from Alpha, Louis married Lucille and immediately began a six-month tour. Lucille joined him on the road so that they could spend Christmas together. But that type of life, moving from hotel to hotel, did not agree with Lucille. When she tired of being on the road, he sent her back to New York to locate a home for them to buy.

Instead of choosing a home in Harlem, as Louis expected, she went to Queens, where she knew a white family that wanted to sell its home. It was a quiet, residential neighborhood, away from the hurley-burley nightlife of Harlem. It was the type of home and location, she reasoned, that a man of Louis's stature deserved.

With Joe Glaser's help, she purchased the home for thirty-nine hundred dollars and did not tell Louis a word about it until the transaction was concluded. It was the home that Louis and Lucille lived in for the remainder of their lives.

With the Depression over and the economy heating up because of World War II, Louis's financial situation improved considerably. Glaser kept him booked almost constantly, but the direction of his career was beginning to shift in another direction. His music took a back seat to his persona as an entertainer. He told more jokes, sang more songs, and impressed his fans as much with his personality as with his trumpet.

Glaser wasted no time getting Louis plugged into the Hollywood scene. Louis had appeared in short films in 1931 and 1932, but Glaser had bigger things in mind, and by the late 1930s and early 1940s Louis was appearing in major motion pictures with stars such as Bing Crosby, Jack Benny, and Ann Miller. Louis's smiling face and accessible humor seemed the perfect antidote to the horrors being inflicted in Europe by Nazi Germany.

As Louis's career was expanding, Lil's life was contracting. Her interest in music waned after their divorce. Upon her return to Chicago, she enrolled in a sewing class sponsored by the Work Projects Administration, a federal agency that organized public works to relieve national unemployment. Taking the class was not a haphazard decision, for she had plans to become a clothes designer.

When she was not experimenting with her sewing machine, she took trips to Michigan to visit the cottage where she had spent so much quality time with Louis. It was the only place she ever had him completely to herself, without musicians stopping by to smoke marijuana or talk about music.

How poignant it must have been for her to sit on the back steps of that cottage, looking out across the lake that gave Louis so much pleasure. There are few sounds more lonesome that the rhythmic patter of waves lapping against a dock or a wooded shoreline. It must have soothed her soul and devastated her heart, all in the same instant. So much of their life had been built around sounds. The silence of life without him was deafening in its impact against her heart and soul.

Now in her forties, "Hot Miss Lil" still had the same old sparkle in her eyes, but middle-age had not been kind to her, expanding her body and sagging her self-image. She looked ordinary as she walked the streets of Chicago and she felt ordinary as she went about the daily chores of life. She could have returned to music, the opportunities were still there in Chicago, but her heart just wasn't in it.

Instead, she opened a restaurant at 3406 South State Street. Named Lil Armstrong's Swing Shack, it offered a soul-food menu that consisted of "Boogie-Woogie Stew," "Flat Foot Floogie (pig feet)," "Rug Cutter's Roast and Dipsy Doodle Noodles," "Hamburg Swingaroo," "Bob-cat Fish," "Jam Session Pies," "Tutti-Frutti Inner Tubes (chitterlings)," and "Down Beat Beans (red)."

The restaurant also offered breakfast specials such as "Tisket Biscuits and Tasket Hash" and "Killer Diller Waffles" with "Divine Swine (ham or bacon)." Her advertising motto was: "Come out and beat your chops on our swing food. Our meals are a solid sender right in the groove."

When she was not at the restaurant, she was in a workshop she had set up after completing her WPA sewing class. There she worked to bring life to the clothing designs she sketched out with pen and paper. Once she had the design completed she purchased ready-made patterns similar to her designs and adopted them to the size she wanted for her patterns. From that point it was a simple matter to pin the paper patterns to the fabric she wished to use and then to cut the fabric along the pattern lines. The result was an assortment of fabric pieces that she sewed together to make the final garment.

Lil's designs targeted women and men, although the men's designs were meant for one man in particular—Louis Armstrong. She created suits and jackets specifically for use on the stage. Louis wore her creations with great pride and happily accepted Lil's new role as his private clothes designer.

It had been several years since her divorce from Louis, but Lil still wore the wedding rings he gave her, she still looked for him the first thing in the morning, and she still looked for ways to be a part of his life. Whenever she saw photographs of Louis wearing her clothing, it made her feel closer to him.

When she thought she was ready, she held a fashion show in New York to launch her new line of clothing. World War II was still raging and it was unusual to hold such an event, especially when the guest of honor was a woman of color. There was champagne and music, and people attended to meet "Hot Miss Lil" as much as to examine her new line of clothing. Not surprisingly, Lil was asked to perform for the guests.

One of Lil's creations, a cocktail gown she had named "Mad Money," ended up doing quite well, but America was not yet ready for a black clothes designer. It would be another twenty years before a black model would even be accepted by the industry.

That occurred on June 29, 1962, when *Life* magazine published a story on twenty-three-year-old model Liz Campbell, daughter of cartoonist E. Simms Campbell. The headline on the magazine cover read: "Beautiful Negro model makes a high-fashion breakthrough." The story went on to explain that Campbell was only the second black model in history to be accepted by top New York designers.

Once again, Lil the visionary was ahead of her time. Her career as a clothing designer was doomed to failure because of the racial climate that permeated the industry. No matter how good her designs were, there was simply no possibility that white buyers would purchase the clothing for their white customers.

Lil returned to Chicago with yet another dream shattered.

In the summer of 1944, the New York office of the FBI, as part of an espionage investigation, contacted Louis's manager Joe Glaser. There is no indication in the bureau's files that they realized the extent of Glaser's connections to organized crime figures in Chicago. What the bureau wanted from him was information about a light-colored, redheaded female singer named Bricktop.

She was not suspected of wrongdoing, but agents felt she could give them information about a black, Paris-based trumpet player who was suspected of collaborating with the Nazis. Glaser told agents he would help locate her, but he apparently never offered them any tangible assistance.

Encouraged by the attention Hollywood was paying Louis, manager Joe Glaser relocated to Los Angeles and set up an office at 8278 Sunset Boulevard under the name of Associated Booking, Inc. He had branched out with dance bands and vaudeville acts— and an occasional starring act like Billie Holiday—but he was careful to explain to new clients that Louis always came first.

For some reason, Glaser came under investigation by Retail Credit Company during that time. In a report that ended up in the Chicago Crime Commission files, investigators found that he had a net worth of about sixty thousand dollars and an annual income of twelve thousand dollars. Apparently, they found that unusual because he lived in a wealthy Beverly Hill neighborhood and employed a bodyguard and two female servants.

Investigators also noted that his wife was reported to be related to Walter Winchell, "noted columnist, and according to neighborhood sources, probably is a niece to this well-known man."

The first movie role that Glaser got for Louis after his relocation in Los Angeles was *New Orleans,* a United Artists film set in 1917, the year the Storyville district was shut down. For the project, the studio hired Glaser's top two, A-line clients—Louis Armstrong and Billie Holiday. Studio executives proclaimed it to be a real jazz movie with real jazz musicians.

New Orleans turned out to be not as advertised—Holiday was asked to play the role of a house maid and Louis was asked to play a character that had little to do with the real Louis Armstrong— and the final result was a tepid, inaccurate look at New Orleans's contributions to the birth of jazz. With the exception of Louis's performances, *New Orleans* was panned by the critics and ignored at the box office.

For the remainder of the decade, Glaser kept Louis out on the road. There were few low or high points in Louis's career during that time, just a series of one-nighters that seemed to be unending. Not until February 1949 did something come along that really made Louis excited about being a performer. He was asked by the Zulu Social Aid and Pleasure Club in New Orleans to be its "king" during the annual Mardi Gras parade.

For Louis, honors just didn't come any bigger than being acclaimed "King of the Zulus." He told reporters that he was "ready to die" now that he had reached that pinnacle. Mayor DeLesseps Morrison greeted Louis upon his arrival in the New Orleans and in his speech made reference to Louis's "ready to die" statement.

Louis responded with typical good humor: "Yes, Mayor, I do remember saying those words, but it ain't no use for the Lord taking me literally."

That evening, at a performance by Louis and his band at the Booker T. Washington Auditorium, there was a commotion when a brash, hot-tempered woman who identified herself as Mrs. Louis Armstrong crashed the proceedings and demanded free admittance. It was none other than Louis's first wife, Daisy Parker.

Told about the scene that was developing at the front door, Louis peered at the proceedings from a distance and then instructed authorities to allow Daisy into the concert. That evening, two of Louis's wives, Lucille and Daisy, basked in the adulation heaped upon the man they both loved.

Not in attendance were his other two former wives, Alpha and Lil. But in her own way Lil *was* there, for throughout the Mardi Gras festivities Louis wore the magnificent midnight-blue tuxedo she had designed especially for the occasion. Lil took her victories as she could get them, usually in small increments.

After the closing of her restaurant and the failure of her clothing design enterprise, Lil decided to become a teacher. She taught French. She taught piano. She taught music in general. Aside from that, her main vocation throughout the 1940s was making suits for Louis, but even that grew tiresome by the end of the decade.

Jazz had changed greatly since the Hot Fives first recorded in 1925. A new generation of jazz fans had come of age, and they viewed Louis and Lil as old-fashioned relics of another era. Louis was still very much in demand, but more as a comedian and entertainer than as a legendary musician. Through attrition, his high-powered band, the All Stars, gradually became the so-so stars, primarily because Joe Glaser began hiring less expensive (and less experienced) sidemen for Louis's shows.

In the early 1950s, Lil was largely unknown, for it had been more than a decade since she had released any records or performed in any high-profile venues. Dissatisfied with her life, she decided to return to music. Since there were few opportunities for her in the United States, she did what so many other blues and jazz artists did— she went to Europe to perform before grateful audiences that had not forgotten her contributions to American music. She spent most of 1952 and 1953 in Europe, primarily in France and Poland, and she even did some recording for a French record label while there.

In December 1952, she participated in Paris's "Jazz Month" celebration. Two major concerts were scheduled for the centuries-old Salle Pleyel, followed by a "Grand Night of Jazz" at the Coliseum. New Orleans clarinetist Sidney Bechet, who had recently bought a nightclub in Pigalle, was the headliner at the first concert, and Lil and trumpeter-singer Peanuts Holland headlined the second concert.

The following spring she had a brief reunion with Louis in Paris. Hearing that he was in town for a concert, she went to the hotel where he and Lucille were staying. Interrupting his morning shave to greet Lil, he made a real event out of the visit by hugging and kissing her with the shaving cream still caked on his face.

With Lucille looking on with obvious approval, Lil smiled, as only Louis could make her smile, relishing the moment, to the delight of a photographer who snapped a photograph that was published in newspapers around the world.

In September 1953, Lil left Paris and returned to the United States. Hearing applause again had invigorated her and reminded her of her true mission in life, but she found few opportunities back in the United States. For one thing, race had become an issue in ways that had seemed nonexistent or unimportant in the 1920s and 1930s. In the aftermath of World War II, race relations had deteriorated as black leaders had begun to press for legal and social reforms.

Also affecting the opportunities available to Lil was the changing face of American music. Jazz had become, more or less, a private club for white male musicians. They made most of the records and they reaped most of the benefits. The black musicians who played jazz, like trumpeter Dizzy Gillespie and saxophonist Charlie Parker, preferred a less structured style of playing like bebop. Typically, they would begin a song with a recognizable melody, then break it down into free-flowing cascade of notes, harmonies, and alter-rhythms, painting a more abstract image with their notes.

That was not the type of music that Lil performed. How odd it must have seemed to both "Hot Miss Lil" and "The Greatest Trumpet Player in the World" that the art form they had created and nurtured had moved on to something else that no longer required their services as mentors.

Now in her mid-fifties, Lil found work as a musician in Chicago, but it was primarily as a novelty act, someone who could perform the "oldies but goodies" of another era. Louis was facing much the same problems, only on a grander scale. He coped by recording and playing cover songs in his act that were familiar to his white audiences. To be fair to Louis, it was not entirely the sell-out it appeared to be. He enjoyed all types of music, and when he heard something on the radio that struck his fancy he worked it up for his nightclub and concert audiences.

In 1956 Louis had his biggest chart hit to date with the release of "Mack the Knife" from the stage musical *A Threepenny Opera*. It was not the sort of music you would expect from the greatest trumpet player in the world, but it was popular and it helped pay the bills and those types of considerations had their place in his life.

Actually, the older Louis got, the more apparent Lil's early influence on his career became. Louis and Lil argued in later years about the authorship of many of their collaborations—it was the only time in his life that Louis ever made negative public comments about Lil—but the fact remains that Lil increased her song output after their separation and Louis decreased his, to the point where it eventually stopped altogether.

Left to his own devices, Louis early on shunted his instrumentalist talents aside in favor of becoming a stage personality, something he had wanted during his early years with Lil.

Aside from his Top 20 hit with "Mack the Knife," Louis's greatest impact on the 1950s was with the public position he took on the issue of school desegregation. It all began with television coverage of the school desegregation crisis in Little Rock, Arkansas. Governor Orval Faubus had called out the National Guard to block court-ordered school desegregation.

Louis was in Grand Forks, North Dakota, for a performance when he saw images on television of fearful black children being taunted and heckled by hateful white adults. With a reporter in his hotel room he lost his temper. "The way they are treating my people in the South, the government can go to hell," he said, referring to an upcoming trip organized for him by the State Department. "It's getting so bad, a colored man hasn't got any country." Ranting to the reporter, he called President Dwight Eisenhower "two faced" and he described Faubus an an "uneducated plow boy."

The FBI already had a secret file on Louis (FBI director J. Edgar Hoover had an obsessive dislike of African Americans), one that contained comments about him using marijuana. But when his comments about Little Rock hit the news wire, agents took note of everything that was said and done in the weeks that followed.

When Eisenhower responded to the crisis by sending troops to Little Rock to enforce the court order, Louis changed his mind about the president. This time, he applauded Eisenhower and said his actions made the United States the "greatest country" in the world. He also said he might change his mind about his trip overseas for the State Department.

There is no question about the sincerity of Louis's stand on the desegregation issue, but his opinion did not develop in a vacuum. Two events occurred prior to that that helped push him over the edge. The first was an incident in Knoxville, Tennessee. While he was on stage playing "Back O' Town Blues," someone tossed a dynamite bomb over the fence that surrounded the auditorium. The blast tore a five-foot hole in the ground and send a shock wave through the auditorium.

Louis told reporters, "I've been playing the horns for forty-four years and never had any trouble before." Police told him it was probably related to bombings in nearby Clinton, Tennessee, where bombs had destroyed the homes of thirty black families. "Where's Clinton?" Louis asked. "I'll blow anywhere. The horn doesn't know anything about these race troubles."[3]

The second event that disturbed Louis was a newspaper story about Louis's upcoming trip overseas for the State Department. Government officials told the reporter that Louis's two-week trip to Buenos Aires would not cost American taxpayers a penny since the musician was receiving twenty thousand dollars a week from his host country.

The newspaper story went on to explain that while Louis worked for free, other jazz musicians had received substantial subsidies from the government. Louis's competitor, Dizzy Gillespie, for example, was paid $133,000 for a trip to the Middle East and Benny Goodman was paid $135,000 for a trip to the Far East.

The way Louis saw it, if he was willing to work free of charge for the United States, the very least the government could do in return was protect black children whose only crime was wanting an education.

The decade ended with a flourish for Lil, with Ray Charles's 1959 remake of her song, "Just for a Thrill." It appeared on *The Genius of Ray Charles* album, one many critics consider among his most influential. Other songs on the album included

"Don't Let the Sun Catch You Cryin'," "Let the Good Times Roll," and "It Had to Be You."

Only twenty-seven at the time the album was recorded, Charles was an enigma to many critics. To Nat Hentoff, coeditor of *The Jazz Review*, he was a jazz singer who was breaking new ground in popular music.

"There have been very few singers in jazz who could shout the blues convincingly and be just as at ease in softer stories, " wrote Hentoff in the liner notes. "There have been even fewer who could fuse a band together from the piano at the same time."

Charles's version of Lil's song introduced her music to a new generation of music lovers that appreciated the sophisticated way she blended lyrics with melody. For a song to work for Lil, it had to have words that carried the listener into the melody line. She accomplished that with "Just for a Thrill," a fact recognized by the many artists who subsequently recorded the song, including Peggy Lee, Nancy Wilson, the Ink Spots, Aretha Franklin, and the J. Geils Band.

Regardless of who records the song, it is difficult to listen to it and not think of Lil and Louis, and of the deep pain and the lofty joy and optimism the relationship brought to Lil. She wrote about what she knew and understood, which is what every writer should do in any medium.

The Last Song Is Always the Best

On February 3, 1961, Lil turned sixty-one. She had gained weight since the early days of her career, when her eighty-five pounds of fiery energy on the bandstand had never failed to create a stir. Now most of the fire was in her eyes, which as often as not were set off with a tinge of mischievousness. Say something in her presence that was incorrect or beyond the bounds of reason, and she would put you in your place with The Look, a penetrating gaze that never needed words to complete her thought.

Lil still performed, but not often. When she did, it was almost always for nostalgia buffs. Gone were the days of being on the cutting edge. What she and Louis had created had evolved into something else entirely. That in itself is neither good nor bad, but it does raise questions about the proper roles of innovators in American society once the spark of their genius has been handed off to longer distance runners.

In Lil's case, she had one last album to record before calling it quits. Riverside Records had begun a series of recordings titled "Chicago—The Living Legends." Lil was asked to be the focus of the third album in that series.

Lil took three songs of her own to the session, which took place on September 7, 1961, at The Birdhouse recording studio in Chicago. The idea was to put her with two groups of veteran jazzmen, but when a previously scheduled session with Earl Hines ran longer than expected and reduced the time they had for Lil's session, the producer Chris Albertson decided to combine the two bands.

Lil was on piano, of course, but the trumpet section consisted of Bill Martin, Roi Nabors, and Eddie Smith; Preston Jackson and Al Wynn, trombones; Darnell Howard and Franz Jackson, clarinets; Pops Foster, bass; and Booker Washington, drums.

All of the musicians had impressive resumes, but not everyone was currently making a living as a musician. Bill Martin drove a cab when he wasn't performing with a band. Roi Nabors worked as a laboratory technican. Preston Jackson had once played with Carroll Dickerson at the Sunset and at Dreamland Café, but now operated his own produce business. Of those working full-time as musicians, most were current members of Earl Hines's band. That included Eddie Smith, Darnell Howard, and Pops Foster.

To Albertson, Lil was "without a doubt, the most vivacious jazz performer [he] had ever come across." He found it difficult to believe that the spry lady sitting on the piano bench in the studio had once occupied the same seat forty years earlier with King Oliver's Creole Jazz Band.

As always, Lil reported to the session with songs of her own— "Boogie Me," "Eastown Boogie," and "Clip Joint," a song she wrote in 1939 but had never recorded. The first song on the album, "Royal Garden Blues," is strictly an ensemble piece. Smith, Preston Jackson, and Howard start it off, with Nabors, Wynn, and Franz

Jackson following in close pursuit. Almost everyone does a solo, including Lil, whose right hand does things never heard on the early Hot Five recordings.

"Red Arrow Blues" is a bluesy New Orleans–type instrumental with lots of slide in the trombones and clarinets that talk back to the drums all the way through the piece. There is some stop-time action in the song, but it is a pale imitation of Louis's best work. A big finish with smooth drum work wraps it up just fine.

Kid Ory's "Muskrat Ramble" turned into a free-for-all as everyone jumped in and grabbed a piece of the action. Lil does more on the piano than she did on the original and the trumpet work never finds the subtlety Louis injected into it, but the crystal-clear high notes provide the saving grace. At the end of the song, with the tape still running, there is a Lil "moment" as she shouts "now tape it," only to be informed by the engineer that they had been recording all along (the band had thought it was a practice run-through).

"Boogie Me" is a duet with Lil at piano and Washington on drums. It comes the closest of anything she ever recorded of showing what she was probably like at her own piano in her home. Her hard-banging left hand is evident throughout the piece, but for the first time she shows what she can do with her right hand. Of special interest are some right-handed riffs, repetitive flurries, that are reminiscent of the ones Dave Brubeck made famous in the late 1950s and early 1960s. The question is, did Lil pick them up from Brubeck, or was she playing them all along? If it is the latter, that truly paints an interesting picture of what the creative process was like for Lil and Louis when they were alone in their home working on the songs that made stars of the Hot Fives.

"Clip Joint" is the only song on the album that features Lil doing a vocal. From a big, low-down opening with tom-toms, Lil launches into taunting vocal that is followed by a series of solos from trumpet, clarinet, and trombone. On the other side of the bridge, Nabors joins Lil with a series of growling answers to her vocal. Although sixty-one, Lil sounds full of vigor and every bit of twenty.

"Basin Street Blues," probably one of the most recognizable jazz songs of all time, opens with some splendid trombone work by Al Wynn. Preston Jackson follows with a trombone solo that is equally engaging. Despite that, the song never really gels.

The third of Lil's songs, "Eastown Boogie," begins with Lil on the piano and Washington on the drums, setting a steady but challenging pace for the other instrumentalists who enter one at a time, each taking turns keeping up with Lil. The song was named after a bar in Milwaukee where Lil performed in 1942.

The final song, "Bugle Blues," provides, as the title suggests, an opportunity for the trumpets to lead the way through a maze of wind-up solos that never pause once they kick into the song. Washington provides an excellent drum solo of the type that was then in vogue with jazz-leaning rock 'n' roll bands.

All in all, the album offered forty minutes of Lil at her best, working with a group of seasoned professionals who performed the music to 1960s standards, not necessarily the way it had been done in the 1920s. It would prove to be Lil's last collection of music.

The end of the 1950s and the beginning of the 1960s were nothing but trouble for Louis's manager Joe Glaser. The dynamiting in Tennessee, Louis's comments about the government's treatment of blacks, school integration in Little Rock—all had taken a toll in the late 1950s, all the more so since few black leaders supported Louis's stand against racism. Southern promoters canceled concerts when they learned that Louis had a racially mixed band. One of Glaser's other clients, Dave Brubeck, also ran into trouble for the same reason. Cancellations are a fact of life in the booking business, but when extraneous issues like racism figure into the equation, it creates new stresses.

On top of all that, Glaser had to contend with an aging client base that was becoming more susceptible to diseases associated with old age and the long-term problems associated with various addictions. Whereas once all he had to do was fight for his clients, now he had to comfort them and hold their hands as they traveled through the valley of death. No one would have ever confused the tough-talking Glaser for a social worker, but playing that role was now part of his job description.

That became apparent in 1959 when Billie Holiday, his favorite client next to Louis, entered a downward spiral in her addiction to cocaine and alcohol. Always plump and fleshy, her weight went down to less than one hundred pounds; with her head rolling and spit trickling down her chin, she sometimes had to be lead on stage to perform.

Glaser tried to persuade her to check into a hospital, but she refused, saying that was a luxury she could not afford. Glaser promised he would pay for her hospital bill, but she still would not seek medical treatment. On May 30, 1959, one day before a scheduled appearance in Montreal, Canada, she collapsed and went into a coma.

Holiday was taken to Knickerbocker Hospital in New York, but when medical personnel at the private hospital examined her, they found needle tracks on her arms and the smell of alcohol on her breath. They diagnosed her as being a drug addict and alcoholic and transferred her to a public facility, Metropolitan Hospital. When her physician tracked her down, he found her on an unattended stretcher in a hallway.

Holiday's condition made news, of course, and Glaser assured reporters that he would take care of all her bills. "We've been together since she was fifteen," he said. "I'm taking care of everything."[1] Unknown to Glaser, a rival persuaded Holiday to sign with another manager while she was semiconscious in the hospital.

Eleven days after her admittance to the hospital, nurses found traces of cocaine that had been smuggled in to the singer. The police were called and Holiday was fingerprinted and photographed for a mug shot. Glazer intervened and obtained legal counsel for her, blocking attempts to send her to the Women's House of Detention, but the case never went through the court system because the singer died on July 10.

When Glaser checked into her finances, he discovered she was in even worse shape than he had imagined. She had a little over four hundred dollars in cash and owed twenty-five thousand dollars to her record company. Her total net worth was just $1,345.36.[2]

It was not until after Holiday's death that Glaser learned that she had signed with another manager during the same week that he had agreed to pay her hospital expenses. Of course, paying the bills of a loyal, recovering client was different than paying the bills of a disloyal, penniless client, so he never said much more about the bills once Holiday was buried.

Dying clients took an emotional toll on Glaser, but they were really the least of his problems. In the aftermath of President John F. Kennedy's assassination in Dallas, Texas, Glaser was drawn into that investigation because of his association with Jack Ruby, the Dallas nightclub owner who murdered Kennedy's assassin on live television.

Interviewed by FBI agents about his relationship with Ruby, who had known mob connections to the Chicago underworld, Glaser described Ruby as a "phony" and a "name-dropper." He said Ruby once tried to hire an employee of Louis's, but the request was denied. FBI agents accepted Glaser's comments at face value and then moved on.

By that time, FBI agents were aware of Glaser's association with the Chicago mob. His name arose several times on wiretaps of Murray "The Camel" Humphreys, who headed the old syndicate once controlled by Capone. By the time FBI agents interviewed Glaser in 1963, they were fully aware that Associated Booking had been taken over by the same underworld organization suspected of involvement in the Kennedy assassination.[3]

It was not until 1966 that Glaser's mob ties made national news. The story began with a heavyweight championship fight that was scheduled between Mohammed Ali, who then fought under the name Cassius Clay, and Ernie Terrell. The fight was canceled when New York boxing officials learned of Terrell's association with Bernard Glickman, a boxing promoter and associate of some of the nation's top hoodlums.

When that happened, Glickman was attacked by a mob enforcer who handcuffed Glickman and almost choked him to death. Glickman went to the FBI and turned state's evidence against the mob. In the federal probe that followed, Joe Glaser was among the high-profile witnesses who were called to testify before the grand jury in Chicago.

What he told the secret panel is not known, neither is his relationship with the principles in the case. Although it is clear from Glaser's FBI file that he had a close association with the mob, that part of his file has been blackened out by FBI censors.

Louis had known about Glaser's mob connections from the very beginning (it was the reason he wanted him as his manager), but there is no evidence that Louis knew that a portion of his earnings was ever channeled back into the Chicago organization. Louis probably would not have cared, even if he had known, although that should not be construed as approval of the mob's activities. According to a former band member, Louis grinned broadly whenever he was around known gangsters, but never

missed an opportunity to express his true feelings while performing for them.

He did that by mixing in repetitions of "kiss my ass, kiss my
ass" among his nonsensical scat choruses. Not understanding a
word he was saying, the gangsters would gaze back with admiration
and applaud. Despite his "Uncle Tom" image, he never believed
that whites were intellectually superior to blacks.

In the mid-1960s, Chris Albertson, who had produced the
Living Legends album with Lil, approached her about cowrit-
ing her autobiography. Both were neophytes when it came to writing a book, but he was able to persuade her to begin work on the
project. According to Albertson, he was able to obtain a publishing
contract for the book.

In many ways, Albertson was an unlikely writing partner for
Lil. Born in Reykjavik, Iceland, he had studied art in Copenhagen
before immigrating to the United States in 1957. He had never lived
in the South and knew little about the culture that created jazz.
What he did have was a passionate interest in jazz, so much so that
he was able to land a job as a radio disk jockey in Philadelphia.

Lil and Albertson worked together for a while, but then she
broke off their relationship. Albertson told this author that it was
because she felt the book would paint too intimate a portrait of
Louis and she had second thoughts about writing it—and that was
probably what she told him.

More likely, she simply found that the collaboration was not
working for her, perhaps because of their cultural differences, for
she continued to work on the book without Albertson. By 1969, she
had completed work on four chapters, according to correspondence
with Francis Squibb, a professor at the University of Alabama.

Squibb suggested that she work with an experienced cowriter, but she rejected that idea. "Most of the writers and reporters that have interviewed me from time to time change or distort the facts and that is the main reason that I want no help from anyone," she wrote. "Of course, that doesn't mean that I won't accept constructive criticism as [sic] enlarge or cut-down on some subjects."

Lil informed Squibb that she planned to self-publish her book, and he apparently cautioned her about signing agreements with potentially unscrupulous publishers. Lil responded that she was not too concerned about that. "My idea was to have a few hundred copies and use my mailing list along with the other people that keep bugging me for this book," she wrote. "I am not writing a statistical book (so many people have done a very good job along that line). . . . I plan only to write about my personal experiences with the various musicians, especially those that I worked with and made records."[4]

By the late 1960s, Lil was in a retrospective frame of mind. What little performing she did was not significant financially, but it did keep her in contact with the public, and that was becoming increasingly important to her. For the first time, perhaps, she began to realize the importance of what she and Louis had accomplished as a team.

In a 1968 interview with John S. Wilson for the *New York Times*, she reminisced about the early days in Chicago. "If you want to hear Louis really play," she said, "just get him to play when he's angry."[5] It was a line she had used a hundred times before and it always got the attention of whatever reporter or jazz writer she was talking to at the time. Interviews, for her, had become like songs, with a beginning, a bridge, and an end.

At the time of the interview, Lil was in New York to perform at the Top of the Gate. It was the first time she had performed in

New York since 1957 when she appeared at Jimmy Ryan's for two weeks with the Cecil Scott band.

Writing about Lil, Wilson said she was, at sixty-five, "a hearty woman with a bubbling personality, who plays piano and sings with a zest and assurance that completely belie her age." Completely taken by "Miss Lil"—she told him that she preferred that over "Mrs. or Miss Armstrong"—Wilson described her performance as a "romping pianistic spirit and a vocal style that ranged from literal lyrics to bubbling happy matters."

A few weeks later, while performing in New Orleans, she did another interview in which she reminisced about the old days in Chicago, only this time she focused on Jelly Roll Morton. Interestingly, she confided that before she started performing again on a regular basis, she went back and relearned all of Morton's solos. "Before, I never played any of Jelly's stuff, only the band things, you know," she said. "But now I know four or five of his solos . . . and they're very, very effective as solos. You don't have to—I don't add anything to them, [just] play them just like they're written."[6]

For the last ten years of his life, Louis Armstrong coasted as a musician. Glaser kept him moving along at a brisk pace, but the projects that gave him the highest profile were his travels abroad for the State Department and his novelty recordings. His long simmering transition from musical innovator to entertainer was, at long last, complete.

Ironically, the biggest hit of Louis's career was a Broadway show tune. When he first recorded "Hello, Dolly!" it was done as a demo at Glaser's request. It was just one of several show tunes for his latest album. The Broadway show of the same name had already opened, but Louis, or "Satchmo," as he was then calling himself, knew nothing about it. He recorded the song, then left the mainland to perform in Puerto Rico.

Much to Louis's surprise, the song shot up the charts, finally reaching the number one position on May 9, 1964. Not since "Mack the Knife" had he recorded such a popular song. At the age of sixty-three, he became the oldest recording artist to ever have a number one hit.

Even more surprising was the fact that "Hello, Dolly!" knocked two Beatles' songs out of contention, "Do You Want to Know a Secret?" and "Can't Buy Me Love." It was easily the best-selling record of Louis's career. When the movie was made, he sang the song to the film's leading lady, Barbra Streisand, thus increasing his profile even higher, especially among a new generation that had never heard of Louis Armstrong or the music he had made famous.

As a result of the success of "Hello, Dolly!" Louis recorded an entire album of show tunes titled *What A Wonderful World*, the title song of which became a hit twenty years later when it was included in the soundtrack of the movie *Good Morning, Vietnam*.

Unfortunately, accompanying Louis's surge in popularity in the mid- to late 1960s was a corresponding decline in his health. All those years of eating fatty foods, smoking marijuana, and avoiding physical exercise finally caught up with him.

In September 1968, he went to his doctor's office to talk to him about a shortness of breath he was experiencing; but before the doctor could see him, Louis changed his mind and left. Instead, he decided to ignore the symptom, even when his ankles swelled, hoping that it would all simply go away. It didn't. In February 1969 he was hospitalized for two months for treatment of heart and kidney problems.

While he was in the hospital, Joe Glaser suffered a stroke in the elevator in his office building. He was taken to the same hospital where Louis was being cared for, but no one told Louis about Glaser immediately for fear it would jeopardize his health. When Louis learned of Glaser's condition he asked to see him, but he was disappointed by the visit, for Glaser was in a coma and did not recognize him. Glaser never awoke from the coma and died on June 6, 1969.

To a friend, Louis wrote: "It was a toss-up between us who would cut out first. Man it broke my heart that it was him. I love that man, which the world already knows. I prayed, as sick as I was, that he would make it. God bless his soul. He was the greatest for me—all the spades that he handled."[7]

Louis recovered from his bout with heart and kidney failure, at least well enough to go home, but the incident had left him in a frail condition. He resumed his performing and recording schedule, although on a limited basis. His last performance was a two-week engagement at the Waldorf-Astoria's Empire Room in New York. He did it against doctor's orders, saying that he had to do it since music was his life.

Exhausted by the engagement, he was again hospitalized for several months. When he was allowed to leave the hospital in mid-June, he went home and immediately began making plans for another tour. On July 6, 1971, he died in his sleep in his own bed.

Lil was devastated by Louis's death. She had known it was coming—*everyone* knew it was coming—but that did nothing to lessen the impact of the loss. They had been more than husband and wife; they had been musical soulmates. Their marriage had produced no children, but it had produced a form of music that the world was calling America's greatest contribution to the arts, the country's only truly original music.

Lil went to the funeral, where she stood in line with everyone else, including Lucille and Louis's sister Beatrice, to view his body at a funeral home in Corona. His body was then moved to the Seventh Regiment's armory in Manhattan for public viewing. He was dressed in a black silk suit and a pink shirt with a pink and blue necktie. The white handkerchief that he always displayed when he played was in the coffin beneath his hand, but his trumpet was not. Lucille held onto that as a keepsake.

Three days later, on July 9, a service was held at Corona's Congregational Church. About five hundred people attended, including Dizzy Gillespie, Guy Lombardo, Benny Goodman, Duke Ellington, Ella Fitzgerald, Johan Jones, Gene Kruppa, New York Governor Nelson Rockefeller, Mayor John Lindsay of New York, and Leonard Garment, a White House adviser sent by President Rickard Nixon.

The service was simple. Singer Peggy Lee, wearing a black gown, sang "The Lord's Prayer," and Al Hibbler sang "Nobody Knows the Trouble I've Seen" and "When the Saints Go Marching In."

During the service, Lil complained to those around her that she was not feeling well. Everyone thought it was probably the stress of saying goodbye to Louis.

Outside the church, more than one thousand fans gathered to listen to the service over loudspeakers. Millions more watched and listened on television. After the service, Louis was buried in Flushing Cemetery, where young girls fought for the red roses in the funeral wreaths.

Writing in *Newsweek*, Hubert Saal described Louis as the person who "pretty nearly invented jazz, transforming entertainment into an art of intense expressiveness, imposing order on what was chaos." About his own death, Saal quoted Louis as saying, "When I get to the Pearly Gate I'll play a duet with Gabriel.

Yeah, we'll play 'Sleepy Time Down South.' He wanted to be remembered for his music just like I do. You have to have something to die with."

After the funeral service, Lil returned to Chicago. She had said goodbye to Louis a hundred times before, but always with the expectation of seeing him again someday. This time was different. The last time is always different.

At age seventy-three, she was now totally alone in life. Louis was her last link with the real world. They had had no children. She had no brothers or sisters. Indeed, her only family members, cousins mostly, were back in Memphis, a long way from the life she knew in Chicago.

Unable to find closure, Lil went to the cottage in Michigan. It was the only place left where she could *feel* his presence. There on a hot July day, with no one around to overhear her parting words, she said goodbye to Louis, the only man she ever loved.

Seven weeks later, on August 27, 1971, Lil was invited by Chicago's Reach Out program to participate in a memorial concert for Louis at the Civic Center Plaza. More than two thousand jazz fans and downtown office workers gathered for the high-noon concert, many with box lunches. Everyone was in a celebratory mood.

On that day it was a comfortable sixty-eight degrees, with bursts of bright sunshine ricocheting off the buildings around the plaza. There had been a trace of rain earlier in the day.

Among those in the audience was *Chicago Tribune* jazz critic Harriet Choice. When she spotted Lil sitting in the shade awaiting her cue to take the stage, she went over to talk to her. They had become friends in recent years. On several occasions, Choice had spent her birthdays at Lil's house at 421 East Forty-Fourth Street.

"She would play anything I asked," Choice recalled. "She was fun to be with, and she could make a good mess of greens. The thing that I remember the most is that she would sometimes haul out a letter from Louis."[8]

At the plaza, Choice knelt down beside Lil's chair and asked if she could interview her. "We'll talk later, honey," said Lil, who was wearing a brightly colored print dress and silver slippers. Chimes rang out in the plaza, causing everyone to look around for the source of the music. No one could figure out where the chimes came from. It was a mystery.

There had been several tribute speeches about Louis, but a chorus was singing when the chimes first rang out. The music was supplied by a band led by Red Saunders. Choice knelt beside Lil's chair, honoring her request to be left alone. She admired her greatly. "I liked hearing her play 'The Pearl' and 'Maple Leaf Rag,' she said. "Purists would have hated the way she played those songs, but I loved it."

Suddenly, Lil shivered. "I'm chilly," she complained. "I hope I get to play before those chimes sound off again."

Lil got her wish. Moments later, she was introduced to the audience by the master of ceremonies. Without fanfare, she sat down on the piano bench, her slender hands reaching out from over-sized sleeves to play W. C. Handy's "St. Louis Blues." It was a song that brought her full circle from her Memphis roots.

The members of the audience, some of whom were only seated about ten feet away, cheered and broke out into smiles. Lil herself was grinning broadly, her eyes sparkling from the energy she received from the audience. She played the song loudly and forcibly, as was her custom, her hands seemingly doing battle with the keyboard.

Then came the final moment of the song, a loud, ringing chord that was held until the last resonance of the song could be heard.

Lil paused, her hands still on the keyboard, then she toppled over onto the concrete floor. There was a gasp from the audience.

For a moment, everyone on stage simply froze. Then someone rushed forward and rolled her over onto her back to give her mouth-to-mouth resuscitation. But it was too late: Lil Hardin Armstrong had died of a broken heart at the age of seventy-three.

Within moments paramedics arrived. They slipped off her silver slippers and loosened her clothing. They did everything they could to revive her, but it was to no avail. She was loaded onto a stretcher and carted away. As they were leaving, the chimes sounded again. Choice thought, "Well, she got her wish!"

The people on stage and the audience quickly scattered. After Lil had given her life to Louis, what else was there to say in tribute? All that remained on stage was the piano and a pair of silver slippers. . . . *and those chimes!*

 Lil was pronounced dead on arrival at Wesley Memorial Hospital.

Funeral services were held on Tuesday, August 29, 1971, in the chapel of a funeral home at 3232 South King Drive. It was a hot, stormy day, with the temperature hovering around ninety degrees.

Unlike Louis's funeral, which had been attended by hundreds and viewed on live television by millions, only a handful of mourners showed up for Lil's funeral and most of them were neighbors from her Forty-Fourth Street address.

There was no eulogy from the musicians she had worked with in the early years because she had outlived them all. The service was not even attended by members of the Chicago news media, except for Harriet Choice—and she was there out of personal friendship, not because her editors asked her to attend.

There were no mayors or governors or representatives of the president at Lil's service, but notices of her death appeared in newspapers around the country. Noticeably absent from the stories were comments from old friends and admirers, and assessments by leading jazz figures of her place in history.

Lil simply disappeared from the jazz scene, with barely a ripple.

Not until several years later, when books were published on the life of Louis Armstrong and other jazz pioneers did comments about Lil begin to surface in print. Old friend and admirer Jonah Jones said, "I thought this was a most wonderful woman."

John Hammond wrote, "One of the most lovable people that ever existed in music was Lil Hardin Armstrong, Louis's wife and protector during those early rough days in Chicago. Lil was saintly and kind and no match for the vultures who surrounded Louis in the most creative days of his career."[9]

Preston Jackson said, "She is due a lot of credit. I feel that if it wasn't for Lil, Louis would not be where he is today."[10] Of Lil's divorce from Louis, Alberta Hunter, said sadly upon Lil's death, "She never got over it."[11]

When it comes to American music, Lil accomplished more than any women before or after her arrival on the scene. She was a true visionary. She coinvented jazz with Louis Armstrong, she taught him how to become a virtuoso performer, she composed over one hundred and fifty songs, she received two advanced degrees in music, she learned French, she became a clothes designer, and she was a successful band leader and recording artist.

Throughout all her successes and failures, she remained true to her own moral vision and, in doing so, she became a role model for how to achieve goals in life while remaining true to one's self. Her downfall was also her main strength in life: Her undying devotion to the only man she ever loved, Louis Armstrong.

Postscript

After Lil was buried, vultures descended upon her house. Carted away were her letters, the manuscript of her autobiography, photographs, her personal effects, and perhaps even Louis's first cornet. To this day, none of those effects have surfaced, except for a letter from Louis that was once auctioned off to an unidentified private collector.

A check of the various jazz archives around the country revealed no trace of Lil's materials. Michael Cogswell, director of the Louis Armstrong House and Archives, says he has often wondered about the whereabouts of the missing materials.

I would like to locate those missing materials and return them to Lil's rightful heirs. Anyone with information about their whereabouts or information about possible heirs to Lil's estate is encouraged to contact me at Lilarmstrong98@cs.com.

Lil has relatives, most likely living in north Mississippi or west Tennessee, but I have been unable to locate them. Their last names would be Hardin or Martin, but could have changed through marriage. They will know they are related to Lil if they can trace their own family lineage back to William or Dempsey Hardin, or Taylor or Priscilla Martin.

More than artifacts are at stake. While doing research for this book, I discovered that, with one minor exception, no one has collected the royalties for Lil's songs since 1971. The one exception is a woman named Barbara Kight, who is indicated on publisher's records as a beneficiary for royalites on a handful of songs. All letters to Ms. Kight were unanswered and all attempts to locate her were unsuccessful.

The amount of money that would be due the heirs of Lil Hardin Armstrong is confidential with the publishers, but with recordings of her work from everyone from Ray Charles to Frank Sinatra to Louis Armstrong, it may be assumed that a sizable fortune is at stake. I will assist any rightful heirs, without compensation, in their efforts to lay claim to Lil's fortune and artifacts. If you have helpful information, please write to me in care of my publisher or contact me at the above e-mail address.

Recommended Recordings

Lil Hardin Armstrong and Her Swing Orchestra
Classics Records (564)

Lil Hardin Armstrong/Chicago—The Living Legends
Riverside Records (OJCCD-1823-2)

Louis Armstrong/The Hot Fives and Hot Sevens
Volume III
Columbia Records (CK 44422)

Louis Armstrong/The Hot Fives and Hot Sevens
Volume II
Columbia Records (CK 44253)

Louis Armstrong/The Hot Fives
Volume I
Columbia Records (CK 440049)

Louis Armstrong/Hot Fives and Sevens
4 CD set
JSP Records (314)

The Genius of Ray Charles
Atlantic Records (1312)

Partial List of Songs by Lil Hardin Armstrong

Just For A Thrill (recorded by Ray Charles, Nancy Wilson, Peggy Lee, the Ink Spots, J. J. Johnson, Milt Jackson, Ray Brown, Lou Donaldson, Jimmy Dorsey, and Helen O'Connell)

Struttin' With Some Barbecue (recorded by Louis Armstrong, Pete Fountain, Al Hirt, Jack Teagarden, Pee Wee Russell, Billie Holiday, Clarence Williams, Earl Hines, Willie Nelson, Rampart Street Jazz Band, Dukes of Dixieland, Bobby Hackett, Lu Watters, Benny Goodman, Doc Severinsen, The Gene Krupa Orchestra, Paul Desmond, Bob Crosby, and others)

Perdido Street Blues (recorded by Louis Armstrong, Frank Sinatra, Johnny Dobbs, and others)

I'm Not Rough (recorded by Louis Armstrong, The J. Geils Band, and others)

King of the Zulus

Where Were You Last Night?

You're Next

You Run Your Mouth

Skit Dat De Dat

Sweet Lips

Tears

Tomorrow Night
Too Tight Blues
Two Deuces
When I Went Back Home
Knee Drops
Let's Get Happy Together
Lonesome Blues
Mad Dog
My Sweet Lovin' Man
Once in a While
Papa Dip
Satchel Mouth Swing
Bad Boy
Clip Joint
Don't Jive Me
Flat Foot
Goover Dance
Got No Blues
Happy Today, Sad Tomorrow
Heah Me Talkin'
Hi De Ho Man
Hotter Than That
I Can't Say
Jazz Lips
New Orleans Stomp
Brown Gal
It's Murder
I'm Knockin' At The Cabin Door
Everything's Wrong, Ain't Nothing Right
Born To Swing
Let's Call It Love
Lindy Hop
My Secret Flame
Eastown Boogie
Boogie Me

Notes

See bibliography for publication information for sources.

CHAPTER 1

1. John E. Harkins, *Metropolis of the American Nile*, p. 45.

2. Joseph Blotner, *Faulkner: A Biography*, pp. 12–13.

3. Shelby Foote, *The Civil War: A Narrative*, p. 518.

4. Allen Cabaniss, *The University of Mississippi: Its First Hundred Years;* Robert B. Highsaw and Charles N. Fortenberry, The Government and Administration of Mississippi.

5. William Faulkner, *The Unvanquished*, p. 85.

6. George W. Lee, *Beale Street: Where the Blues Began.*

7. Frank Taylor, *Alberta: A Celebration in Blues.*

8. John E. Harkins, *Metropolis of the American Nile.*

9. Clark Porteous, *Memphis Press-Scimitar*, April 28, 1976.

10. Lil Hardin Armstrong on Riverside CD.

11. C. Robert Tipton, "The Fisk Jubilee Singers," *Missionary Herald*, September 1947.

CHAPTER 2

1. *Chicago Tribune*, April 1918.

2. Charles Reagan Wilson and William Ferris, editors, *The Encyclopediua of Southern Culture.*

3. F. Scott Fitzgerald, author of *The Great Gatsby*. Gatsby was a wealthy New Yorker with a vague but suspect background who longed to be accepted into polite society.

4. Robert J. Schoenberg, *Mr. Capone.*

5. Williams Research Center, New Orleans, Louisiana.

6. Ibid.

7. Ibid.

8. Lil Hardin Armstrong on Riverside CD.

9. *American Women in Jazz.*

10. *Jazz: A History of America's Music.*

11. Baby Dodds, *The Baby Dodds Story.*

12. *Louis Armstrong: In His Own Words.*

13. Laurence Bergreen, *Louis Armstrong: An Extravagant Life.*

14. *Down Beat*, June 1, 1951.

15. Lil Hardin Armstrong interview on Riverside CD.

16. Ibid.

CHAPTER 3

1. Laurence Bergreen, *Louis Armstrong: An Extravagant Life.*

2. Williams Research Center.

3. Ibid.

4. Frank Taylor, *Alberta Hunter: A Celebration in Blues,* p. 35.

5. P. L. Prattis, *Pittsburgh Courier*, September 2, 1961.

6. Mary Letts, *Al Capone* (1974)

7. Robert J. Schoenberg, *Mr. Capone.*

8. *Mafia*, Time-Life Books.

9. Lil Hardin Armstrong interview on Riverside CD.

10. Ibid.

11. Baby Dodds, *The Baby Dodds Story.*

12. Ibid.

13. James Chilton, *Louis.*

14. Ibid.

15. *Jazz: A History of America's Music.*

16. *The Baby Dodds Story.*

17. *Louis Armstrong.*

18. Ibid.

19. *Jazz: A History of America's Music.*

20. Louis Armstrong in His Own Words/Louis Armstrong House and Archives at Queens College/CUNY.

CHAPTER 4

1. Max Jones and John Chilton, *Louis: The Louis Armstrong Story*, 1971.
2. *Louis Armstrong, in His Own Words.*
3. *The Baby Dodds Story.*
4. Lil Hardin Armstrong interview on Riverside CD.
5. Ibid.
6. *Louis.*
7. Lil Hardin Armstrong interview on Riverside CD.
8. *Louis Armstrong, in His Own Words.*
9. Ibid.
10. Ibid.
11. Ibid.
12. Lil Hardin Armstrong interview on Riverside CD.
13. *Louis.*
14. Lil Hardin Armstrong interview on Riverside CD.
15. Sam Tanenhaus
16. Lil Hardin Armstrong interview on Riverside CD.
17. Lil Hardin Armstrong interview on Riverside CD.
18. Ibid.
19. *The Baby Dodds Story.*
20. *Louis Armstrong, in His Own Words.*
21. *Louis.*
22. Lil Hardin Armstrong interview on Riverside CD.
23. Ibid.
24. *Louis Armstrong.*

CHAPTER 5

1. Louis Armstrong in His Own Words.
2. *Louis.*
3. Lil Hardin Armstrong interview on Riverside CD.
4. *Louis Armstrong, in His Own Words.*
5. Louis Armstrong Archives.
6. Lil Hardin Armstrong interview on Riverside CD.
7. Ibid.
8. *Louis Armstrong, in His Own Words.*
9. Ibid.
10. Ibid.
11. Louis Armstrong Archives.
12. Rex Stewart, *Jazz Masters of the Thirties.*

13. Lil Hardin Armstrong interview on Riverside CD.
14. Bergreen, per unpublished book.
15. *Louis Armstrong, in His Own Words.*
16. Ed Kirkeby, *Ain't Misbehavin'.*
17. *The Baby Dodds Story.*
18. Goffin Notebooks, Louis Armstrong Archives.
19. Ibid.
20. Lil Hardin Armstrong interview on Riverside CD.

CHAPTER 6
1. Lil Hardin Armstrong on Riverside CD.
2. *Louis.*
3. *Louis Armstrong, in His Own Words.*
4. Lil Hardin Armstrong interview on Riverside CD.
5. *Louis.*
6. Sally Placksin, *American Women in Jazz.*
7. Ibid.
8. Williams Research Center.
9. Chris Albertson, Time-Life booklet.

CHAPTER 7
1. Hogan Jazz Archives, Tulane University, New Orleans.
2. *Louis Armstrong, in His Own Words.*
3. United Press International, February 20, 1957.

CHAPTER 8
1. Stuart Nicholson, *Billie Holiday.*
2. Ibid.
3. *Louis Armstrong.*
4. Letter, Lil Armstrong to Francis Squibb, March 9, 1969, Williams Research Center.
5. John S. Wilson, *New York Times*, December 10, 1968, The Williams Research Center.
6. Interview, January 19, 1969, Williams Research Center.
7. Gary Giddins, *Satchmo: The Genius of Louis Armstrong.*
8. Interview with Harriet Choice.
9. *Saturday Review*, September 25, 1971.
10. Ibid.
11. Frank Taylor, *Alberta Hunter: A Celebration in Blues.*

Select Bibliography

BOOKS

Armstrong, Louis. *Louis Armstrong, in His Own Words*. New York: Oxford University Press, 1999.

Bergreen, Laurence. *Louis Armstrong: An Extravagant Life*. New York: Broadway Books, 1998.

Blotner, Joseph. *Faulkner: A Biography*. New York: Random House, 1974.

Bronson, Fred. *The Billboard Book of Number One Hits*. New York: Billboard Publications, 1985.

Brown, Sandford. *Louis Armstrong*. New York: Franklin Watts, 1993.

Cabaniss, Allen. *The University of Mississippi: Its First Hundred Years*. Hattiesburg, Mississippi: University and College Press of Mississippi, 1949.

Channing, Steven A. *Confederate Ordeal: The Southern Home Front*. Alexandria, Virginia: Time-Life Books, 1984.

Chase, Gilbert. *America's Music: From the Pilgrims to the Present*. New York: McGraw-Hill Book Company, 1955.

Collier, James Lincoln. *Louis Armstrong: An American Genius*. New York: Oxford University Press, 1983.

Couglan, Robert. *The Private World of William Faulkner*. New York: Cooper Square, 1972.

Doyle, Don H. *Nashville: In the New South*. Knoxville, Tennessee: The University of Tennessee Press, 1985.

Editors, The. *True Crime: Mafia*. Alexandria, Virginia: Time-Life Books, 1993.

Faulkner, William. *The Unvanquished*. New York: Vintage Books, 1965.

_____. *The Hamlet*. New York: Vintage Books, 1940.

Fitzgerald, F. Scott. *Six Tales of the Jazz Age and Other Stories*. New York: Scribner, 1960.

Foote, Shelby. *The Civil War: A Narrative*. New York: Random House, 1974.

Gara, Larry. *The Baby Dodds Story*. Baton Rouge, Louisiana: Louisiana State University Press, 1992.

Garon, Paul, and Garon, Beth. *Woman With Guitar: Memphs Minnie's Blues*. New York: Da Capo Press, 1992.

Giddins, Gary. *Satchmo: The Genius of Louis Armstrong*. New York: Da Capo Press, 2001.

Green, Stanley. *Ring Bells! Sing Songs!: Broadway Musicals of the Thirties*. New Rochelle, New York: Arlington House, 1971.

Handy, W. C. *Father of the Blues: An Autobiography*. New York: Da Capo, 1941.

Harkins, John E. *Metropolis of the American Nile*. Oxford, Mississippi: Guild Bindery Press, 1991.

Herzhaft, Gerard. *Encyclopedia of the Blues*. Fayetteville, Arkansas: University of Arkansas Press, 1992.

Highsaw, Robert B., and Charles N. Fortenberry. *The Government and Administration of Mississippi*. New York: Thomas Y. Crowell, 1954.

Jones, Max, and John Chilton. *Louis: The Louis Armstrong Story, 1900-1971*. Boston: Little, Brown and Company, 1971.

Kerr, Elizabeth M. *Yoknapatawpha: Faulkner's "Little Postage Stamp of Native Soil."* New York: Fordham University Press, 1969.

Kirkeby, Ed. *Ain't Misbehavin': The Story of Fats Waller*. New York: Da Capo Press, 1975.

Ladner, Heber. *Mississippi Official and Statistical Register*. Jackson, Mississippi: State of Mississippi, 1980.

Lee, George W. *Beale Street: Where the Blues Began*. College Park, Maryland: McGrath, 1969.

McKee, Margaret, and Fred Chisenhall. *Beale Black and Blue: Life and Music on Black America's Main Street.* Baton Rouge, Louisiana: Louisiana State University Press, 1981.

Miller, William D. *Memphis During the Progressive Era.* Memphis: Memphis State University Press, 1957.

Newman, Ralph, and E. B. Long. *The Civil War (volumes I and II).* New York: Grosset and Dunlap, 1956.

Nicholson, Stuart. *Billie Holiday.* Boston: Northeastern University Press, 1995.

Panassie, Hugues. *Louis Armstrong.* New York: Da Capo, 1979.

Pilkington, John. *The Heart of Yoknapatawpha.* Jackson, Mississippi: University Press of Mississippi, 1981.

Placksin, Sally. *American Women in Jazz: 1900 to the Present, Their Words, Lives, and Music.* New York: Wideview Books, 1982.

Randall, J. G., and David Donald. *The Civil War and Reconstruction.* Lexington, Massachusetts: D. C. Heath and Company, 1969.

Schoenberg, Robert J. *Mr. Capone.* New York: William Morrow,

Schuller, Gunther. *Early Jazz: Its Roots and Musical Development.* New York: Oxford University Press, n.d.

_____. *The Swing Era.* New York: Oxford University Press, 1989.

Thompson, Charles Manfred. *History of the United States.* New York: Benjamin J. Sanborn and Co., 1927.

Tucker, Frank C. *Alberta Hunter: A Celebration in Blues.* New York: McGraw-Hill, 1987.

Ward, Geoffrey C. *Jazz: A History of America's Music.* New York: Alfred A. Knopf, 2000.

Wilson, Charles Reagan, and William Ferris. *Encyclopedia of Southern Culture.* Chapel Hill, North Carolina: University of North Carolina Press, 1989.

Wiltz, Christine. *The Last Madam: A Life in the New Orleans Underworld.* New York: Faber and Faber, 2000.

(unsigned) Fisk University Catalog (1915-1916).

MAGAZINE AND NEWSPAPER ARTICLES

Chastain, Wayne. "Many Hearts, 'Too Sad to Be Blue' Remember Spirit of Beale Street." *Memphis Press-Scimitar* (n.d.).

Choice, Harriet. "Satchmo's Ex-Wife Dies Here." *Chicago Tribune* (August 28, 1871).

Leroux, Charles. "Scarface, shmarface: Think of Capone as a CEO with a Tommy Gun." *Chicago Tribune* (January 15, 1999).

Parks, Gordon. "Swirl of Bright Hues." *Life* (June 29, 1962).

Porteous, Clark. "Handy's House Stands As History's Treasure." *Memphis Press-Scimitar* (April 28, 1976).

Saal, Hubert. "Good-by Louis." *Newsweek* (July 19, 1971).

Sanderson, Jane. "Memphis Slim Brings the Blues Back to Beale Street Where It All Began." *Memphis Press-Scimitar* (March 17, 1978).

Smith, Whitney. "Uncovering the History of Beale Street." *The Commercial Appeal* (February 20, 1983).

Taylor, Henry N. "State Department Digs That Armstrong Jazz." *Scripps-Howard News Service* (1957).

Tipton, C. Robert. "The Fisk Jubilee Singers." *Tennessee Historical Quarterly,* Spring 1970 (Volume XXIX, Number 1).

(unsigned) "Satchmo's Band Is Target of Dynamiting." United Press International (February 20, 1957).

(unsigned) "State Officials Seek Leaders in Alien Lynching." *Chicago Tribune* (April 1918).

_____. "Nude Statue On Art Institute Steps Must Go." *Chicago Tribune* (April 1918).

_____. "Seize 28 Slot Machines Amid Lots of Gun Play." *Chicago Tribune* (January 19, 1918).

_____. "Robertson and Merriam Debate For Negro Vote." *Chicago Tribune* (February 3, 1919).

_____. "People." *Jet Magazine* (May 28, 1953).

_____. "Louis Armstrong's 2nd Wife, Lil Hardin, Dies at a Tribute." *United Press International* (August 28, 1971) as appeared in the *New York Times.*

_____. "Lil Armstrong Services Set Tuesday Night." *Chicago Tribune* (August 29, 1971).

Wiedrich, Robert. "FBI Shields Glickman in Fight Probe." *Chicago Tribune* (March 26, 1966).

Wilson, John S. "Miss Lil Armstrong Reminisces." *New York Times* (December 10, 1968).

Index

Gillespie, Dizzy, 196, 198
Gioia, Ted, 137
Glaser, Joseph (Joe), 109–11,
    131–32, 136, 140, 146, 176–77,
    188–89, 192–93, 204–8; health,
    211–12
Glickman, Bernard, 207
Goodman, Steve, 31
Good Morning, Vietnam, 211
gramaphone, 96–97
Grant, Ulysses S., 5, 6, 23
Great Depression, 157, 169, 172, 175
Griffith, D. W., 159
"Gully Low Blues," 141, 142
"Gut Bucket Blues" (Armstrong,
    Louis), 126–27

Hall, Minor, 59, 70, 72
Hall, Tubby, 52, 59
Hamlet, The (Faulkner), 17
Handy, W. C., 12–13, 16–20, 115, 117
Hardin, Dempsey, 1–3, 11–12, 20–22,
    37–39, 54–55, 57–58, 102–3,
    128, 143–45
Hardin, William, 1–3, 11–12
Harlem, 157
Harlem Harlicans, 171
"Harlem on Saturday Night," 182
Harvey, James, x
"Heebie Jeebies," 130, 139
"Hello, Dolly!", 210–11
Henderson, Fletcher, 80, 113,
    115–19, 171
Hentoff, Nat, 199
Herbert, Stewart, 1
Higginbotham, J. C., 182
Hines, Earl, 132, 136–37, 149–53, 202
Hoijnack, Walter, 33
Holiday, Billie, 192, 193, 205–6
Holland, Peanuts, 195
Hoover, J. Edgar, 197

Hot Fives. *See* Louis Armstrong and
    the Hot Fives
Hot Sevens, 141, 145
Hot Sixes, 150, 151–53
Howard, Darnell, 202
"How Come?", 65
Hugh Hoskin's, 42
Humphreys, Murray "The Camel," 207
Hunter, Alberta, 13, 42, 52, 60–65, 118

"I'll Be Glad When You're Dead, You
    Rascal You," 168
Illinois Central railroad, 31
improvisation, 53
Indiana, 96
instrumentation, 16, 143
Irish, 36

Jackson, Franz, 202–3
Jackson, Preston, 202
Jackson, Tony, 58
James, George, 162
jazz, ix–x, 42–43, 67, 117–18;
    female musicians, x–xii, 51–53,
        70–71, 171, 173;
    white musicians, 195–96
Jazz Age, 117–18, 157
Jazz Review, 199
Jennette Street (Memphis), 12
jitney dance clubs, 72
"Joe Turner Blues" (Handy), 19
Johnson, Bill, 44, 82
Johnson, Jack, 87
Johnson, Jimmy, 64, 71, 83, 86
Johnson, Lonnie, 147
Jolson, Al, 42
Jones, Davey, 70, 72–73
Jones, Isham, 88
Jones, Jennie, 37–38, 51–52
Jones, Jonah, 172, 173, 186, 187
Jones, Polly, 187

About the Author

James L. Dickerson is the author of *Colonel Tom Parker: The Curious Life of Elvis Presley's Eccentric Manager*; *Goin' Back to Memphis: A Century of Blues, Rock 'n' Roll, and Glorious Soul* (both available from Cooper Square Press); *Coming Home: 21 Conversations about Memphis Music*; *That's Alright, Elvis: The Untold Story of Elvis' First Guitarist and Manager* (with Scotty Moore); *Women on Top: The Quiet Revolution That's Rocking the American Music Industry*; and *Dixie Chicks: Down-Home and Backstage*; among many other books. A longtime Memphis resident, Dickerson currently lives in Brandon, Mississippi.

OTHER COOPER SQUARE PRESS TITLES OF INTEREST

COLONEL TOM PARKER
The Curious Life of Elvis Presley's Eccentric Manager
James L. Dickerson
310 pp., 35 b/w photos
0-8154-1088-3
$28.95

GOIN' BACK TO MEMPHIS
A Century of Blues, Rock 'n' Roll, and Glorious Soul
James L. Dickerson
284 pp., 58 b/w photos
0-8154-1049-2
$16.95

UNFORGETTABLE
The Life and Mystique of Nat King Cole
Leslie Gourse
352 pp., 32 b/w illustrations
0-8154-1082-4
$17.95

THE ART PEPPER COMPANION
Writings on a Jazz Original
Edited by Todd Selbert
312 pp., 4 color photos, 12 b/w photos
0-8154-1067-0
$30.00 cloth

WAITING FOR DIZZY
Fourteen Jazz Portraits
Gene Lees
Foreword by Terry Teachout
272 pp.
0-8154-1037-9
$17.95

OSCAR PETERSON
The Will to Swing
Updated Edition
Gene Lees
328 pp., 15 b/w photos
0-8154-1021-2
$18.95

SWING UNDER THE NAZIS
Jazz as a Metaphor for Freedom
Mike Zwerin
with a new preface
232 pp., 45 b/w photos
0-8154-1075-1
$17.95

REMINISCING WITH NOBLE SISSLE AND EUBIE BLAKE
Robert Kimball and William Bolcom
256 pp., 244 b/w photos
0-8154-1045-X
$24.95

HARMONICAS, HARPS, AND HEAVY BREATHERS
The Evolution of the People's Instrument
Updated Edition
Kim Field
392 pp., 44 b/w photos
0-8154-1020-4
$18.95

THE BLUES
In Images and Interviews
Robert Neff and Anthony Connor
152 pp., 84 b/w photos
0-8154-1003-4
$17.95

DREAMGIRL & SUPREME FAITH
My Life as a Supreme
Updated Edition
Mary Wilson
732 pp., 150 b/w photos, 15 color photos
0-8154-1000-X
$19.95

DID THEY MENTION THE MUSIC?
The Autobiography of Henry Mancini
Henry Mancini with Gene Lees
with a new afterword
312 pp., 44 b/w photos
0-8154-1175-8
$18.95

HE'S A REBEL
Phil Spector — Rock and Roll's Legendary Producer
Mark Ribowsky
368 pp., 35 b/w photos
0-8154-1044-1
$18.95

FAITHFULL
An Autobiography
Marianne Faithfull with David Dalton
320 pp., 32 b/w photos
0-8154-1046-8
$16.95

MADONNA
Blonde Ambition
Updated Edition
Mark Bego
416 pp., 57 b/w photos
0-8154-1051-4
$18.95

ROCK SHE WROTE
Women Write About Rock, Pop, and Rap
Edited by Evelyn McDonnell & Ann Powers
496 pp.
0-8154-1018-2
$16.95

ADAM CLAYTON POWELL, JR.
The Political Biography of an American Dilemma
Charles V. Hamilton
576 pp., 36 b/w photos
0-8154-1184-7
$22.95

BLACKFACE
Reflections on African Americans in the Movies
Expanded Edition
Nelson George
330 pp., 23 b/w photos
0-8154-1194-4
$16.95

WESTSIDE
The Coast-to-Coast Explosion of American Hip Hop
William Shaw
334 pp.
0-8154-1196-0
$16.95

AMERICAN WOMEN ACTIVISTS' WRITINGS
An Anthology, 1637–2001
Edited by Kathryn Cullen-DuPont
568 pp., 16 b/w photos
0-8154-1185-5
$35.00 cl.

CLARA BOW
Runnin' Wild
David Stenn
with a new filmography
368 pp., 27 b/w photos
0-8154-1025-5
$19.95

MARGARET SANGER
An Autobiography
New introduction by Kathryn Cullen-DuPont
516 pp., 1 b/w photo
0-8154-1015-8
$17.95

SCOTT FITZGERALD
A Biography
Jeffrey Meyers
432 pp., 25 b/w photos
0-8154-1036-0
$18.95

BLUE ANGEL
The Life of Marlene Dietrich
Donald Spoto
376 pp., 57 b/w photos
0-8154-1061-1
$18.95

Available at bookstores; or call 1-800-462-6420

COOPER SQUARE PRESS
150 Fifth Avenue
Suite 817
New York, NY 10011